# Patterns of Adolescent Self-Image

Daniel Offer, Eric Ostrov,
Kenneth I. Howard,  *Editors*

**NEW DIRECTIONS FOR MENTAL HEALTH SERVICES**

H. RICHARD LAMB, *Editor-in-Chief*

Number 22, June 1984

Paperback sourcebooks in
The Jossey-Bass Social and Behavioral Sciences Series

Jossey-Bass Inc., Publishers
San Francisco • Washington • London

Daniel Offer, Eric Ostrov, Kenneth I. Howard (Eds.).
*Patterns of Adolescent Self-Image.*
New Directions for Mental Health Services, no. 22.
San Francisco: Jossey-Bass, 1984.

**New Directions for Mental Health Services Series**
H. Richard Lamb, *Editor-in-Chief*

**New Directions for Mental Health Services** (publication number
USPS 493-910) is published quarterly by Jossey-Bass Inc.,
Publishers. Second-class postage rates paid at San Francisco,
California, and at additional mailing offices.

*Correspondence:*
Subscriptions, single-issue orders, change of address notices, undelivered
copies, and other correspondence should be sent to Subscriptions,
Jossey-Bass Inc., Publishers, 433 California Street, San Francisco
California 94104.

Editorial correspondence should be sent to the Editor-in-Chief,
H. Richard Lamb, Department of Psychiatry and the Behavioral
Sciences, U.S.C. School of Medicine, 1934 Hospital Place,
Los Angeles, California 90033.

Library of Congress Catalogue Card Number LC 83-82733

International Standard Serial Number ISSN 0193-9416

International Standard Book Number ISBN 87589-779-7

Cover art by Willi Baum

Manufactured in the United States of America

# Ordering Information

The paperback sourcebooks listed below are published quarterly and can be ordered either by subscription or single-copy.

Subscriptions cost $35.00 per year for institutions, agencies, and libraries. Individuals can subscribe at the special rate of $25.00 per year *if payment is by personal check*. (Note that the full rate of $35.00 applies if payment is by institutional check, even if the subscription is designated for an individual.) Standing orders are accepted. Subscriptions normally begin with the first of the four sourcebooks in the current publication year of the series. When ordering, please indicate if you prefer your subscription to begin with the first issue of the *coming* year.

Single copies are available at $8.95 when payment accompanies order, and *all single-copy orders under $25.00 must include payment*. (California, New Jersey, New York, and Washington, D.C., residents please include appropriate sales tax.) For billed orders, cost per copy is $8.95 plus postage and handling. (Prices subject to change without notice.)

Bulk orders (ten or more copies) of any individual sourcebook are available at the following discounted prices: 10–49 copies, $8.05 each; 50–100 copies, $7.15 each; over 100 copies, *inquire*. Sales tax and postage and handling charges apply as for single copy orders.

To ensure correct and prompt delivery, all orders must give either the *name of an individual* or an *official purchase order number*. Please submit your order as follows:

*Subscriptions:* specify series and year subscription is to begin.
*Single Copies:* specify sourcebook code (such as, MHS8) and first two words of title.

Mail orders for United States and Possessions, Latin America, Canada, Japan, Australia, and New Zealand to:
Jossey-Bass Inc., Publishers
433 California Street
San Francisco, California 94104

Mail orders for all other parts of the world to:
Jossey-Bass Limited
28 Banner Street
London EC1Y 8QE

## New Directions for Mental Health Services Series
H. Richard Lamb, *Editor-in-Chief*

# Contents

# Editors' Notes

Adolescents have become increasingly important to mental health practitioners over the past several decades. Thus, more psychiatric units for the treatment of disturbed adolescents have been opened in the United States and in other Western countries during the past two decades than for any other age group, and the literature on the clinical and psychiatric aspects of adolescence has increased geometrically during that period. In the 1950s, Erik Erikson and Anna Freud pioneered the field of adolescent psychology and psychopathology. The interest in adolescents increased dramatically among clinicians beginning with Peter Blos in 1960. *Adolescence*, a journal devoted exclusively to clinical work with adolescents, was established in the 1960s. The American Society for Adolescent Psychiatry was organized in 1967. In 1971, the society started an annual volume, *Adolescent Psychiatry*, which was devoted exclusively to the clinical and psychotherapeutic aspects of adolescent psychiatry. In 1972, the *Journal of Youth and Adolescence* began publication as an outlet for research on adolescence. Since then, many articles and books have been written on different aspects of adolescent psychology and psychopathology. These publications clearly document the great interest that mental health professionals have taken in this subject.

Historically, almost all knowledge about adolescents has been based on adults' experiences with adolescents in clinical or correctional settings. Few attempts have been made to examine the generalizability of the resulting findings. In addition, empirical research on adolescents has often depended on in-depth case reports, and little effort has been made to objectify the criteria for normality and psychopathology. Similarly, attempts to evaluate the results of psychotherapeutic interventions have not been systematic enough. Instrumentation has not been sufficiently reliable and valid to allow careful evaluation either of the adolescent experience or of treatment approaches. In this volume, we will emphasize one reliable and valid psychological instrument, the Offer Self-Image Questionnaire (OSIQ) and show its utility for research on normal and psychiatrically disturbed adolescents. Use of this questionnaire allows us

The editors express their gratitude to Irving B. Harris for his ongoing support of their research and also to the Adolescent Research Team at Michael Reese Hospital and Medical Center: Shiaomay Young, program coordinator; David Parrella, systems analyst; Bruce Briscoe, computer programmer; and Susan Cooper Markovitch, Ming Chow, Tamar L. Offer, and Robert Wolf, research assistants. Merry V. Wilson, research secretary, deserves recognition for her important contribution.

The research reported in this volume was supported in part by the Adolescent Research Fund: In Memory of Judith Offer of Michael Reese Hospital and Medical Center. The editors are grateful to John Stefek, director of the Institute for Juvenile Research, for his continuing support.

1

to focus on one crucial aspect of the adolescent's psychological world, the adolescent's self-image.

Contributions to this volume emphasize aspects of the self-image of both normal and disturbed youth. The first three chapters describe normal adolescents. Chapters One and Two discuss important differences between boys' and girls' self-images in both the junior high school and the high school years. Chapter Three explores the conceptions — and misconceptions — that mental health professionals hold about normal teenagers. The next three chapters describe disturbed adolescents. Chapter Four examines the differences in symptom profile between depressed adolescents and adolescents with conduct disorders. Chapter Five discusses the nature of self in disturbed adolescents. Chapter Six focuses on the self-image of disturbed youths in the community who have yet to be identified as disturbed. Chapter Seven takes a historical perspective, showing trends that may influence adolescents' self-image and behavior. Finally, Chapter Eight traces the implications of all these findings for mental health professionals, teachers, and parents. Those who treat adolescents need to know what adolescents think their world is like. They also need to know what is normal and what is abnormal in adolescent's self-image — and what common misunderstandings mental health professionals have in this regard. This volume will help professionals to differentiate the self-images held by various groups of psychiatrically ill adolescents. Definitions are based on the diagnostic system set forth in DSM-III. Historically, cross-culturally, developmentally, and diagnostically, this volume strives to enrich understanding of the experience of today's adolescents for adults who interact with them, whether in schools, the community, mental health clinics, or the home environment.

Daniel Offer
Eric Ostrov
Kenneth I. Howard
Editors

*Daniel Offer is chairman of the Department of Psychiatry at Michael Reese Hospital and Medical Center and professor of psychiatry at the University of Chicago Pritzker School of Medicine.*

*Eric Ostrov is director of forensic psychology in the Department of Psychiatry at Michael Reese Hospital and Medical Center and research associate (assistant professor) in the Department of psychiatry at the University of Chicago Pritzker School of Medicine.*

*Kenneth I. Howard is professor of psychology at Northwestern University; professor of psychology at Northwestern University Medical School; senior research consultant in the Department of Psychiatry at Michael Reese Hospital and Medical Center; and senior research consultant at the Institute for Juvenile Research.*

*The vast majority of adolescents in the United States and other countries are well adjusted, have good relations with their families and friends, and accept the values of society.*

# The Self-Image of Normal Adolescents

*Daniel Offer*
*Eric Ostrov*
*Kenneth I. Howard*

Very little empirical work was done on normal adolescents until the very recent past. Most clinicians and theoreticians assumed that the normal teenager could be understood by studying psychiatric patients. Thus, the prevalent view has been that adolescence is a time of great stress and turmoil. This storm and stress theory has a long history. Eighty years ago, Hall (1904) stressed the unpredictability of adolescents' moods and behavior. Hall's view has been shared by such theoreticians as A. Freud (1958), Erikson (1959), and Blos (1961). Thus, Gardner (1959) used a disturbed adolescent applying for out-patient psychiatric care to illustrate the depressions, problems, and anxieties that, he claimed confront the normal adolescent. As recently as 1980, Rabichow and Sklansky (1980) claimed that adolescence is more stressful in itself and as full of a variety of problems than any other period in the life cycle.

It seemed to us that the best way to answer the question, What are normal adolescents really like? was to conduct a direct empirical study of normal — in our case, nonpatient — teenagers. First, we completed a ten-year intensive longitudinal follow-up study of normal adolescent boys (Offer, 1969; Offer and Offer, 1975). The data on which we will focus here result from a

D. Offer, E. Ostrov, K. I. Howard (Eds.). *Patterns of Adolescent Self-Image.* New Directions for Mental Health Services, no. 22. San Francisco: Jossey-Bass, June 1984.

large-scale questionnaire study that used the Offer Self-Image Questionnaire (OSIQ) (Offer and others, 1982) as the main data collection device.

## Method

The Offer Self-Image Questionnaire is a self-descriptive personality test that assesses the adjustment of teenage boys and girls between the ages of thirteen and nineteen. It measures the teenager's feelings about his or her own psychological world in eleven content areas.

Since 1962, the questionnaire has been used in more than 120 samples, and it has been administered to more than 20,000 teenagers. The samples included males and females; younger and older teenagers; normal, delinquent, psychiatrically disturbed, and physically ill adolescents; and urban, suburban, and rural adolescents in the United States. The questionnaire has been translated into fifteen languages, and current samples have been collected in Australia, Israel, Ireland, England, India, Venezuela, France, Germany, Italy, Bangladesh, Taiwan, Japan, Holland, Turkey, and Switzerland.

Our particular operational approach rests on two major assumptions. First, it is necessary to evaluate the functioning of the adolescents in multiple areas, since they can master one aspect of their world while failing to adjust in another. Second, the psychological sensitivity of adolescents is sufficiently acute to allow us to use their self-descriptions as a basis for reliable selection of subgroups. Empirical work with the questionnaire has supported both assumptions.

From the beginning, one of our goals was to study a group of adolescents that psychiatric researchers had not previously studied, mentally healthy adolescents. Our study was empirical, not clinical. We wanted to learn from the adolescents what their world was like and how they perceived it. With the questionnaire, we aimed at studying the phenomenal self, the "me" of the adolescent. The 130 items on the questionnaire cover eleven content areas and five different "selves":

| | |
|---|---|
| Psychological Self 1 | Impulse control |
| Psychological Self 2 | Emotional tone (mood) |
| Psychological Self 3 | Body image |
| Social Self 1 | Social relations |
| Social Self 2 | Morals |
| Social Self 3 | Vocational and educational goals |
| Sexual Self | Sexual attitudes and behavior |
| Familial Self | Family relations |
| Coping Self 1 | Mastery of the external world |
| Coping Self 2 | Psychopathology |
| Coping Self 3 | Superior adjustment |

We will not describe in detail the statistical methods used to assure reliability and validity (Offer and others, 1981a). It will suffice to say that the test-retest reliability and the internal consistency of the OSIQ scales are adequate. The vast majority of teenagers took the questionnaire seriously and seemed to enjoy the experience.

We used standard scoring methodology (mean of each scale equals fifty, standard deviation equals fifteen) to analyze and interpret the data. Our 1979 and 1980 samples were used to establish norms ($N = 1,385$). Norms were derived separately for thirteen- to fifteen-year-old males, thirteen- to fifteen-year-old females, sixteen- to nineteen-year-old males, and sixteen- to nineteen-year-old females (Offer and others, 1982). The sample included ten American high schools: five in Chicago suburbs, two parochial schools in Chicago, one rural high school in Minnesota, one high school in Burlington, Vermont, and one private academy in Pennsylvania. In no school did we have less than 85 percent participation. In five high schools, the sample was 98 percent of all the students who attended school on that day. A study of two parochial schools in Chicago and one large suburban high school near Chicago in 1983 yielded standard scores that were virtually identical to those of the norming groups.

## Results

We will present our description of normal adolescents in terms of the five aspects of adolescent self. We will also present results comparing boys and girls, younger and older American adolescents, and adolescents from different generations and cultures.

*The Self-Image of the Normal Adolescent.* As already noted, we conceptualized the self-image of the normal adolescent as consisting of five selves. In the paragraphs that follow, we present the salient characteristics of these aspects of the "me" for the normal adolescent.

*The Psychological Self of the Normal Adolescent.* Our results clearly indicate that it is normal for young people in our culture to enjoy life and to be happy with themselves most of the time. The adolescents whom we studied did not feel that others treated them adversely. Normal adolescents also reported that they were relaxed under usual circumstances. They believed that they could control themselves in ordinary life situations. Anxiety was embedded in a generally strong and positive psychological picture.

In another area, body image, the data indicated that normal adolescents felt proud of their physical development and that the vast majority believed that they were strong and healthy. The implication here is that a positive psychological self complements a feeling of physical health.

*The Social Self of the Normal Adolescent.* The item that received the highest endorsement in the test, "A job well done gives me pleasure," showed the work ethic in its purest form. Judging by the adolescents' responses, that ethic is a universal value in our culture. The adolescents were unreservedly work-oriented. They said that they would be proud of their future profession. It is as if they believed that there were jobs out there waiting to be taken when they were ready to take them. They also stated that they did not wish to be supported for the rest of their lives. As a group, the adolescents in our study saw themselves as making friends easily, and they believed that they would be successful both socially and vocationally in the future.

*The Sexual Self of the Normal Adolescent.* In general, our findings showed that normal adolescents were not afraid of their sexuality. Seven out of ten adolescents stated that they liked the recent changes in their body. Both boys and girls strongly rejected the statement that their bodies were poorly developed. Both boys and girls indicated that they had made a relatively smooth transition to more active sexuality. Nine out of ten subjects said no to the statement "The opposite sex finds me a bore." A majority of the subjects stated that it was important for them to have a friend of the opposite sex.

*The Familial Self of the Normal Adolescent.* Normal adolescents did not perceive any major problems between themselves and their parents. No evidence was presented for major intergenerational conflict. The generation gap so often written about was not in evidence among the vast majority of the teenagers whom we studied. Not only did they have positive feelings toward their parents in the present, they also felt that these good feelings had been true in the past. In addition, they expected that the positive feelings would persist into the future. The most impressive finding in this scale was that eighteen out of nineteen items strongly indicated that adolescents had positive feelings toward their families.

*The Coping Self of the Normal Adolescent.* Normal adolescents were hopeful about their future, and they believed that they could participate actively in activities that would lead them to success. They seemed to have the skills and confidence that they would need for adult life. They were optimistic, and they enjoyed challenges; they tried to learn in advance about novel situations. Normal adolescents had the willingness to do the work necessary to achieve. They liked to put things in order. Moreover, even if they failed, they believed that they could learn from experience.

Normal adolescents denied having the psychopathological symptoms listed in the psychopathology scales. On the whole, they saw themselves as having no major problems. This does not mean that they all said that they did not have problems. A significant minority did not feel secure about their coping abilities. About one in five normal adolescents, our data indicated, felt empty emotionally; these adolescents felt that life was an endless series of problems without a solution in sight. A similar number of adolescents stated that they were confused most of the time. In other words, although most of our subjects stated that they were doers and that they got pleasure from challenges, some were uncertain about what was going on around them and about their capacity to affect the world.

*Sex, Age, and Self-Image of the Normal Adolescent.* Using two-way analyses of variance, we assessed the effects of sex and age on the five selves. Only the major differences will be discussed here. There were no age differences for the psychological self. The sex effects showed that, in general, adolescent girls had significantly more negative feelings about their moods than adolescent boys did. Adolescent girls described themselves as sadder, lonelier, and easier to hurt. They were more sensitive to their internal world than boys were. These findings held both for younger and for older groups. Other items indicated that girls felt ashamed of their bodies, felt ugly and unattractive, and felt less good about recent changes in their bodies more often than boys did. In the areas of self-control, more girls than boys stated that they had fits of crying that they could not control. Adolescent girls affirmed social values much more strongly than adolescent boys did. For example, girls were more concerned with the other person, and they would not hurt another person "just for the heck of it." Girls denied more strongly than boys did that telling the truth meant nothing to them. Although most normal adolescents preferred to work, girls affirmed this value even more strongly than boys did. Boys also showed a more autonomous, less other-directed, and less concerned attitude than girls did. For example, boys affirmed more strongly than girls that they would stop at nothing if someone wronged them. Fewer boys than girls agreed with the statement, "If others disapprove of me, I get terribly upset." In the same vein, more boys than girls said that they felt like leaders. Adolescent girls reported that they were more empathic than adolescent boys. Similarly, adolescent girls felt more attached to their relatives and friends.

Adolescent boys appeared to be more open to their sexual self than girls did. There were no significant age differences. There were no significant differences in age or sex with regard to the familial self. In the coping self, age differences were observed only in that younger adolescent girls described themselves as having more symptoms than older girls did. In general, girls showed more confusion, shame, and fears than adolescent boys did. In general, the girls' faith in their coping abilities was strong but not as strong as that of the boys.

*Generation Change and the Self-Image of the Normal Adolescent.* On the whole, adolescents' self-image was more consistent than disparate across the generations. We did find some differences, and they are significant and noteworthy, but they are only part of the total picture, as Figure 1 shows.

When readers examine the figures in the chapter, they should keep in mind that, in standard score terms, 50 is the mean—that is, normal—and fifteen is the standard deviation. Any score above 50 is above normal, and any score below 50 is below normal. We consider a score of 45 or less to be significantly below normal and a score of 55 or more to be significantly above normal.

In the 1960s adolescents had a more positive psychological self than they did in the 1970s and 1980s. In terms of scale means, all three social self scales showed that teenagers had a more positive social self-image in the early 1960s

## Figure 1. Offer Self-Image Questionnaire (OSIQ)
### Standard Score Profile for American Sample of Normal Male Adolescents
### Twelve to Fifteen Years Old (N = 290)

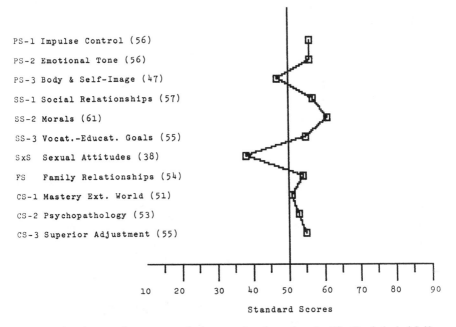

*Note:* Numbers in parentheses are standard score values for each scale. PS = Psychological Self, SS = Social Self, SxS = Sexual Self, FS = Familial Self, CS = Coping Self. Data collected by Offer in two Chicago suburban schools, 1962.

than their counterparts did in the 1970s. It is of particular note that the 1960s subjects had the highest standard score (61) on the morals scale among all the groups that we studied. This indicates that the adolescents of a generation ago had more stable and well-structured ethical standards than their successors. In the 1980s, young people turned inward and showed more concern for themselves. In the 1960s, teenagers had better impulse control and more stable moods than teens in the 1980s, although body image for the latter was similar to that of their peers of the 1960s.

In the 1960s, teenagers described their families in somewhat more positive terms than teenagers used in the 1970s and 1980s. The parents were described as patient, reasonable adults who knew what they were doing. In the 1980s, teenagers were more inclined to say that, although their parents may have been satisfied with them, they were not necessarily satisfied with their parents. The family of the 1980s seemed to be somewhat more distant, and there seemed to be less cohesion and more taking of sides among family members. In the 1960s, parents were seen as more patient and the family as more democratic than they were viewed in the 1980s.

Teenagers of the late 1970s and 1980s more often said that they felt somewhat vulnerable and sensitive. In the 1970s and 1980s, adolescents got more upset if others disapproved of them, and they more often preferred being alone than their counterparts of the 1960s. There were no differences in sexual self between generations. In the coping self, adolescents of the 1960s, 1970s, and 1980s all had similar abilities. (Chapters Seven and Eight of this volume examine the impact of demographic variables on adolescent behavior and self-image.)

The sexual self was the only aspect of self-image in which adolescents of the 1970s and 1980s were significantly more positive than adolescents of the 1960s. These results may be due to increased openness toward sexuality among adolescents of the 1970s and 1980s. In any event, it is of interest that the sexual self is the only part of self-image in which present-day teenagers felt significantly more positive about themselves.

*Cross-Cultural Studies.* The OSIQ has been translated into fifteen languages, and it is currently being used in studies in a number of different countries. It is not our purpose here to treat the cross-cultural studies in depth. We have selected four studies from middle-class high schools in four different countries for illustrative purposes. These studies are not intended to represent the countries or their cultures. They do allow us, however, to compare normal middle-class adolescents from different countries. We have selected only males, since it is beyond the scope of this chapter to include all the different subgroups.

The four Western cultures—Ireland, Israel, Holland, and the United States—exhibit more similarities than they do differences (Figures 1, 2, 3, and 4). It is not until we look at the data for Taiwan (Figure 5) that we see major self-image differences, particularly in symptomatology, sexual attitudes, and the psychological self.

There were some specific cross-cultural differences among the four Western cultures. The Israelis were significantly higher than the Americans on two scales—Morals and Superior Adjustment. As already noted, American adolescents are action-oriented. The Israelis resemble Americans in this respect, but they find the world an even more exciting place than their American counterparts. It is as if Israeli youth were telling us that the more they have to deal with adversity (within limits), the better copers they become. The Dutch teenagers were higher than the American teenagers on three scales—Emotional Tone, Body Image, and Familial Self. The Dutch teenagers felt more emotionally stable and closer to their parents than adolescents in the other countries. The Irish were closest to the Americans in all respects, although they were lower than the American teenagers in Body Image and Mastery. The Taiwanese adolescents were the most perplexing. Like the Israelis, they were significantly higher on the Morals and Superior Adjustment scales. However, unlike the Israelis, they were significantly lower on Impulse Control, Emotional Tone, Body Image, Social Relationships, Vocational and Educational Goals, Sexual Attitudes, Mastery, and Psychopathology. Thus, our data seem to indicate that Taiwanese adolescents are considerably less

12

## Figure 2. Offer Self-Image Questionnaire (OSIQ) Standard Score Profile for Israeli Sample of Normal Male Adolescents (*N* = 87)

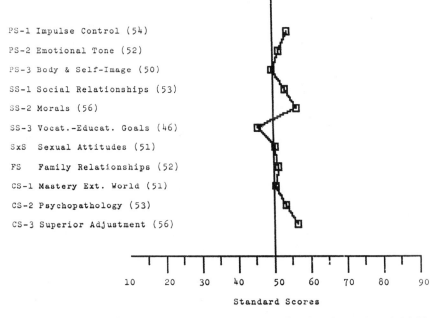

PS-1 Impulse Control (54)

PS-2 Emotional Tone (52)

PS-3 Body & Self-Image (50)

SS-1 Social Relationships (53)

SS-2 Morals (56)

SS-3 Vocat.-Educat. Goals (46)

SxS Sexual Attitudes (51)

FS Family Relationships (52)

CS-1 Mastery Ext. World (51)

CS-2 Psychopathology (53)

CS-3 Superior Adjustment (56)

10  20  30  40  50  60  70  80  90

Standard Scores

*Note:* Numbers in parentheses are standard score values for each scale. PS = Psychological Self, SS = Social Self, SxS = Sexual Self, FS = Familial Self, CS = Coping Self. Data collected by Chigier and Offer, 1974–1976.

confident and self-satisfied than the other adolescents whom we studied. In other words, they have poorer psychological and social selves.

### Discussion

The data that we have reviewed in this chapter reveal a great deal about the phenomenonology of adolescents grouped by age, gender, decade of testing, and country of origin. Normal middle-class adolescents are not in the throes of turmoil. The vast majority of these teenagers function well, enjoy good relationships with their families and friends, and accept the values of the larger society. In addition, most report having adapted without undue conflict to the bodily changes and emerging sexuality brought on by puberty. The only notable symptom that we encountered among normals was a situation-specific anxiety that, Offer (1969) found, normal adolescents can handle without undue trauma.

Age differences were not notable in our normal sample, but sex differences were. Gender, we found, still plays an important role in influencing feelings about body, sexuality, and vocational aspirations. It also plays a large role in orienting persons toward affiliation and morality. We explain these results

**Figure 3. Offer Self-Image Questionnaire (OSIQ) Standard Score Profile for Dutch Sample of Normal Male Adolescents (*n* = 48)**

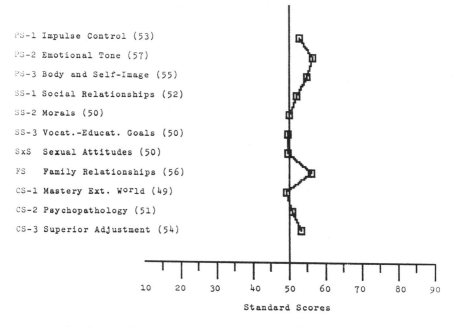

PS-1 Impulse Control (53)

PS-2 Emotional Tone (57)

PS-3 Body and Self-Image (55)

SS-1 Social Relationships (52)

SS-2 Morals (50)

SS-3 Vocat.-Educat. Goals (50)

SxS Sexual Attitudes (50)

FS Family Relationships (56)

CS-1 Mastery Ext. World (49)

CS-2 Psychopathology (51)

CS-3 Superior Adjustment (54)

10  20  30  40  50  60  70  80  90

Standard Scores

*Note:* Numbers in parentheses are standard score values for each scale. PS = Psychological Self, SS = Social Self, SxS = Sexual Self, FS = Familial Self, CS = Coping Self. Data collected by van Leeuven in 1982.

primarily in terms of the traditional sex roles, which exercise their influence either on willingness to admit certain feelings or on orientation to certain areas of mastery, such as individual achievement or interpersonal cohesiveness. Large differences were also found between normal adolescents of the 1960s and normal adolescents of the 1970s and 1980s. Almost all differences, according to our data, indicate that adolescents of the 1960s had greater self-esteem. Three hypotheses can explain these data: Normal adolescents of the 1970s and 1980s were more open to negative feelings than their counterparts of the 1960s; the 1960s generated more positive self-feelings than the 1970s and 1980s; and the formative experiences of adolescents in the 1960s were more conducive to positive self-esteem than the analogous experiences of adolescents in the 1970s and 1980s.

In contrast, the cross-cultural differences were small. They seem to indicate that the experience of adolescence in Western cultures is fairly universal. The differences that did emerge among the cultures that we studied are characterized by a limited set of salient issues, and they are primarily concerned with coping. The dramatic differences between American and Taiwanese adolescents need further study.

Diagnostic work with adolescents has always been difficult (Masterson,

14

### Figure 4. Offer Self-Image Questionnaire (OSIQ) Standard Score
### Profile for Irish Sample of Normal Male Adolescents
### Twelve to Fifteen Years Old (*N* = 163)

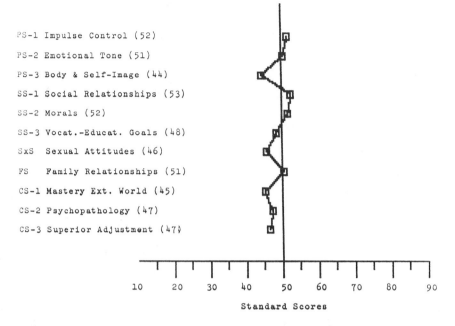

```
PS-1 Impulse Control (52)

PS-2 Emotional Tone (51)

PS-3 Body & Self-Image (44)

SS-1 Social Relationships (53)

SS-2 Morals (52)

SS-3 Vocat.-Educat. Goals (48)

SxS  Sexual Attitudes (46)

FS   Family Relationships (51)

CS-1 Mastery Ext. World (45)

CS-2 Psychopathology (47)

CS-3 Superior Adjustment (47)
```

```
      10    20    30    40    50    60    70    80    90
```

**Standard Scores**

*Note:* Numbers in parentheses are standard score values for each scale. PS = Psychological Self, SS = Social Self, SxS = Sexual Self, FS = Familial Self, CS = Coping Self. Data collected by Brennan in 1976.

1967; Offer, 1969). One part of the difficulty arises from attempts to distinguish serious psychopathology from mild crisis. We can now say, however, that a severe identity crisis and emotional turmoil are just not part of normal growing up. Our belief is that we do not help adolescents who experience such crisis or turmoil when we tell them not to worry about their problems because they are a normal part of adolescence and because they will "grow out" of them. The clinician should be able to diagnose what is presented correctly. He or she can do this only when he or she takes a broad perspective on the varieties of adolescent behavior. In Chapter Five, we discuss the relationships between DSM-III diagnoses and adolescent self-image, and in Chapter Six, we discuss a new category of disturbed adolescent, the quietly disturbed adolescent. We believe that we can help adolescents more if we think of them as individuals first and as adolescents second. Such thinking enables us to isolate an adolescent's problems along the adolescent's developmental lines; it prevents us from referring these problems to "necessities of the age." (Offer and others [1981b] and Chapter Three of this volume address the concepts that mental health professionals have of normal adolescents.)

Adolescence is part and parcel of the human condition. Adults have

**Figure 5.** Offer Self-Image Questionnaire (OSIQ) Standard
Score Profile for Taiwanese Sample of Normal Male Adolescents
Sixteen to Nineteen Years Old (*N* = 70)

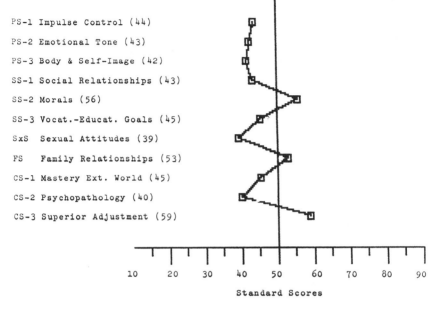

PS-1 Impulse Control (44)

PS-2 Emotional Tone (43)

PS-3 Body & Self-Image (42)

SS-1 Social Relationships (43)

SS-2 Morals (56)

SS-3 Vocat.-Educat. Goals (45)

SxS Sexual Attitudes (39)

FS Family Relationships (53)

CS-1 Mastery Ext. World (45)

CS-2 Psychopathology (40)

CS-3 Superior Adjustment (59)

10    20    30    40    50    60    70    80    90

**Standard Scores**

*Note:* Numbers in parentheses are standard score values for each scale. PS = Psychological Self,
SS = Social Self, SxS = Sexual Self, FS = Familial Self, CS = Coping Self. Data collected
by Turner in 1981.

suffering, psychological traumas, and tragedies, and adolescents do, too. We
are not saying that the modal group for normal American adolescents studied
during the past eighteen years has been functioning on an optimal level; we do
not believe that we are idealizing its members. We believe that adolescents
have conflicts and problems and that they sometimes exhibit disruptive behavior. We believe that our data show clearly that adolescents have the potential
of being happy, of relating well to their peers, parents, and others, and of coping well with their external and internal environment.

The expectation that we adults have of the younger generation should
take into account what the adolescents themselves experience. As we have
seen, the data collected directly from normal adolescents are significantly
different from what adults have assumed that teenagers feel about themselves.
In a way, adolescents are the world's most perfect projective device for adults.
Whatever unfulfilled dreams and fantasies adults have had for their own lives,
they can project onto their children, with the hope that the young will achieve
what they have not been able to achieve. From another perspective, we can
speculate that the growing young represent to their elders their own inevitable
demise. Freud (1955 [1913]) speculated that the conflict between the generations is continuous, although it takes a variety of forms.

In summary, we have presented data on the self-image of a large number of adolescents. We have stressed three things. First, we used self-administered questionnaires to collect our data. Most important, our data are consistent within themselves, and they are congruent with results obtained from use of other psychological instruments such as interviews or parents' evaluations of their children. Second, we found that the normal groups of adolescents whom we studied were characterized more by their similarities than by their differences. The continuity of values for all our samples over an eighteen-year period was especially impressive. We are aware of certain deficiencies in our study, the most important being the omission of representative samples of lower-class and minority group adolescents. The conclusions that we have drawn must be examined with this limitation in mind. Third, we have stressed the diversity of adolescents' view of their psychological worlds. We have presented normal youths to the professional and the lay reader. These youths define normal functioning and development. They reside in our community, and before we can help their disturbed peers who need professional help, we need to know what the norm is. Only then can we correctly diagnose and successfully treat the adolescents who do seek our help.

## References

Blos, P. *On Adolescence: A Psychoanalytic Interpretation.* New York: Free Press, 1962.

Erikson, E. H. "Identity and the Life Cycle." *Psychological Issues,* 1959, *1* (entire issue).

Freud, A. "Adolescence." *Psychoanalytic Study of the Child,* 1958, *13,* 255–278.

Freud, S. "Totem and Taboo." In J. Strachey (Ed.), *Complete Psychological Works of Sigmund Freud.* Vol. 13. London: Hogarth Press, 1955. (Originally published 1913.)

Gardner, G. "Psychiatric Problems of Adolescence." In S. Ariett (Ed.), *American Handbook of Psychiatry.* New York: Basic Books, 1959.

Hall, G. S. *Adolescence: Its Psychology and Its Relation to Physiology, Anthropology, Sociology, Sex, Crime, Religion, and Education.* New York: Appleton, 1904.

Masterson, J. F., Jr. *The Psychiatric Dilemma of Adolescence.* Boston: Little, Brown, 1967.

Offer, D. *The Psychological World of the Teenager: A Study of Normal Adolescent Boys.* New York: Basic Books, 1969.

Offer, D., and Offer, J. B. *From Teenage to Young Manhood: A Psychological Study.* New York: Basic Books, 1975.

Offer, D., Ostrov, E., and Howard, K. I. *The Adolescent: A Psychological Self-Portrait.* New York: Basic Books, 1981a.

Offer, D., Ostrov, E., and Howard, K. I. "The Mental Health Professional's Concept of the Normal Adolescent." *Archives of General Psychiatry,* 1981b, *38,* 149–152.

Offer, D., Ostrov, E., and Howard, K. I. *The Offer Self-Image Questionnaire for Adolescents: A Manual.* (3rd ed.) Chicago: Michael Reese Hospital, 1982.

Offer, D., and Petersen, A. C. "Adolescent Research." *Journal of American Academy of Child Psychiatry,* 1981, *21* (1), 86–87.

Rabichow, H. G., and Sklansky, M. D. *Effective Counseling of Adolescents.* Chicago: Follett, 1980.

*Daniel Offer is chairman of the Department of Psychiatry at Michael Reese Hospital and Medical Center and professor of psychiatry at the University of Chicago Pritzker School of Medicine.*

*Eric Ostrov is director of forensic psychology in the Department of Psychiatry at Michael Reese Hospital and Medical Center and research associate (assistant professor) in the Department of psychiatry at the University of Chicago Pritzker School of Medicine.*

*Kenneth I. Howard is professor of psychology at Northwestern University; professor of psychology at Northwestern University Medical School; senior research consultant in the Department of Psychiatry at Michael Reese Hospital and Medical Center; and senior research consultant at the Institute for Juvenile Research.*

*Of nine areas of adolescent self-image, five change positively,
two remain stable, and two decline during the early
adolescent years.*

# Changes in Self-Image During Early Adolescence

*Robert H. Abramowitz*
*Anne C. Petersen*
*John E. Schulenberg*

A central question in the study of adolescence is whether this time of life is
inherently tumultuous. The view that adolescence is a time of storm and stress
dates back to Hall (1904) and it is supported by such eminent theorists as
A. Freud (1958), Blos (1962), and Deutsch (1967). This view, which is based
on psychoanalytic principles, has been confirmed largely by studies of adolescents in treatment, who represent a small and atypical population of youth. By
contrast, large-scale studies of adolescent development that focused on the
normal adolescent population have concluded that turmoil is relatively
uncommon (Douvan and Adelson, 1966; Offer and Offer, 1975; Rutter and
others, 1976). For example, Offer and Offer (1975) categorized the development of boys between the ages of fourteen and twenty-two as continuous,
surgent, or tumultuous. Only 22 percent of their sample fit into the category of
tumultuous development, which involved anxiety, depression, mood swings,
lack of self-confidence, and distrust, and just one third of the tumultuous
group had received some sort of counseling or therapy (Conger and Petersen,
1984).

The research reported in this chapter was supported by grant MH 30252/38142
from the National Institute of Mental Health to A. Petersen.

D. Offer, E. Ostrov, K. I. Howard (Eds.). *Patterns of Adolescent Self-Image.* New Directions
for Mental Health Services, no. 22. San Francisco: Jossey-Bass, June 1984.

While it is questionable that problems are inevitable in adolescence, it is clear that adolescence remains a potentially stressful period of life. Although the processes that mark the passage from childhood to adolescence occur in different domains of functioning, they can be characterized as discontinuous, demanding, and often difficult for the young adolescent to master (Abramowitz and Asp, 1983). The onset of puberty, transition to a new school structure that makes new demands, increased peer involvement and influence, and the beginning of movement toward some measure of independence from parents occur almost simultaneously, and they alter profoundly the relative simplicity and peace of childhood (Hamburg, 1974). Moreover, abstract and reflective thought about the external world and the self are made possible by increased cognitive capabilities (Inhelder and Piaget, 1958). All these changes require young adolescents to adapt in the way they view themselves — as friend, son or daughter, student, and teenager.

Thus, if early adolescence is a time of deep and demanding changes and of consequent stress, we may ask why it is not more disruptive than studies indicate. Coleman (1978) has attempted to reconcile the classical view of storm and stress with the empirical portrayal of calm and stable adjustment. His focal theory asserts that adolescents avoid stress by coping with one transition at a time. For most adolescents, transitions are not debilitating, because the adaptation process is spread over a number of years. In support of this view, a study by Kokenes (1974) found that, between sixth and eighth grades, a different concern was paramount in young adolescents' minds each year: self-rejection in sixth grade, concerns about peer relations in seventh grade, and family concerns in eighth grade. When disturbance occurs, it is a result of having to manage multiple areas of change at once, and therefore it can be expected to be limited to the period in which transitions overlap (Coleman, 1978).

The effect of developmental changes on early adolescent adjustment can better be understood by considering how adolescents view themselves as they pass through this period. Self-attitudes and evaluations are central constructs in both developmental and clinical research, because they mediate between experience and adjustment (Gecas, 1982). Thus, self-concept is a useful indicator of the potential stress of early adolescent development. This chapter asks whether the multiple transitions of early adolescence make it a disturbing time that has negative consequences for self-concept. To answer this question, we will review the literature and present findings from our own longitudinal study that bear on the question of disturbance in self-image during early adolescence.

## Self-Image: Construct and Definition

Self-views have been defined in several ways. The terms *self-concept* and *self-image* have been used interchangeably (Petersen, 1981) to refer to a phenomenological organization of individuals' experience and ideas about themselves in all aspects of their life (Coombs, 1981). While both self-image and self-esteem are generally conceptualized on a positive-to-negative continuum, self-esteem is a unidimensional, global measure of self-acceptance, whereas self-image approaches multidimensionality. Rosenberg (1979, p. 7) defined self-image as "the totality of the individual's thoughts and feelings having reference to the self as an object." If we adopt this definition, we can speak about various aspects of an individual's self-image — for example, as student, family member, or friend — as well as about how the self-image is manifested in psychological functioning — for example, as impulse control, mental health adjustment, or ease in new situations (Offer and others, 1981). Self-image is not markedly different from self-esteem, but it provides a more detailed and specific assessment of how positively individuals view themselves in various domains of life. In fact, some theorists of self (Rosenberg, 1965; Sherwood, 1965) conceptualize the relation between self-image and self-esteem as an equation in which the various evaluations of self-image dimensions are summed according to weights determined by the personal salience of these dimensions. Self-esteem is the result. Thus, the evaluative aspects of self-image can be considered identifiable and meaningful partitions of self-esteem.

## Review of the Literature

With these definitions in mind, we now turn to the literature on development of self-image in early adolescence. As in all social science research, inferences about adolescent self-image vary with the methods, sample, and questions used. Studies that used a factor-analytic technique to focus on the underlying structure of self-image from childhood through adolescence suggest that there are no discontinuities in dimensions of self-image over time (Dusek and Flaherty, 1981; Michael and others, 1975; Monge, 1973). That is, while average scores on self-image measures can change with age, the underlying structure, represented by the interrelationships among items, appears to be stable over early adolescence.

Longitudinal studies that examined changes in average self-image scores over time have tended to find modest increases in self-esteem in early and midadolescence (Kaplan, 1975; McCarthy and Hoge, 1982; O'Malley and Bachman, 1983) and to find disturbance only in specific subsamples (Blyth and others, 1983). By contrast, cross sectional investigations, which study different subjects of different ages at one time, have produced findings suggesting that self-esteem declines in early adolescence. Piers and Harris (1964) found that sixth-graders scored lower than third-graders and tenth-graders on a 100-item self-description scale. Other investigators (Jorgenson and Howell, 1969; Katz and Zigler, 1967) have reported increasing divergence between real and ideal self-image as children mature into early adolescence. This suggests that young adolescents see themselves as less like the person they desire to be than younger subjects do.

The research of Simmons and her colleagues has provided much basic knowledge on this question. An initial cross sectional study of early adolescence

(Simmons and others, 1973) reported decreased self-esteem, increased self-consciousness, and instability of self-image; all seemed to be associated with entrance into junior high school. A second study designed to investigate this possibility followed students from sixth through tenth grade in two school structures (the twelve grades distributed among schools as six–three–three or as eight–four. This study (Simmons and others, 1979) indicated that the transition to junior high school between sixth and seventh grades is especially detrimental to self-esteem, grades, and participation in extracurricular activities for girls, and it is even more debilitating to self-esteem for girls who have also experienced puberty and begun dating.

The predictions from Coleman's (1978) focal theory concerning the disruptive effect of simultaneous transitions are supported for early-adolescent girls. Possibly because their experience of the events of adolescence is compressed — they experience puberty and begin dating earlier than boys do — girls enter adolescence with less self-esteem and more self-consciousness than boys of the same age (Rosenberg and Simmons, 1975; Simmons and Rosenberg, 1975). Hence, the work of Simmons and her colleagues suggests that early-adolescent self-esteem undergoes a disturbance under specific circumstances — more so for girls than for boys. The school transition explanation of disturbance is consistent with focal theory, as it asserts that the stress of adapting to a new and usually less supportive social environment at a time when other developmental transitions are occurring is especially detrimental (Blyth and others, 1983).

Since young adolescents experience transitions in a number of domains, we may ask whether all aspects of self-image are disturbed by the transition in the same way. Perhaps some aspects of self-image, such as those related to social relations, are not as disturbed as others, such as those related to school or appearance. A unidimensional measure of self-esteem cannot provide information on the various aspects of early-adolescent psychological and social functioning, which may show different responses to the demands of this period. Our study addressed this issue by using a multidimensional self-image questionnaire. The instrument tapped multiple aspects of adolescent life, including psychological functioning, family and peer relations, school, and appearance.

## Study Design and Sample

The study reported here is part of a larger investigation of biopsychosocial development in early adolescence (Petersen, 1983a, 1983b; Petersen and others, 1983; Tobin-Richards and others, 1983), which uses a longitudinal cohort-sequential design (Baltes, 1968; Schaie, 1965) to collect data on boys and girls as they move from sixth through eighth grade. The 254 subjects in our sample (114 boys, 140 girls) were drawn at random in the late 1970s from two consecutive cohorts of sixth-graders in two predominantly white, middle- to upper-middle-class suburbs of a major midwestern city. These subjects were followed from sixth grade to eighth grade. Each year, subjects completed the Self-Image Questionnaire for Young Adolescents (SIQYA), an adaptation of the widely used Offer Self-Image Questionnaire; a few items were modified in order to make the instrument more appropriate for younger subjects (Schulenberg and others, 1984). The instrument contained ninety-eight items. Response values ranged from one to six. Scale scores are calculated in the item metric, with items recoded so that a higher score across all items indicates more positive self-image. The SIQYA consists of nine scales: Impulse Control, Emotional Tone, Body Image, Social Relations, Family Relations, Mastery of the External World, Vocational-Educational Goals, (Less) Psychopathology, and Superior Adjustment. The scales have high reliability (median alpha coefficient: .79 for boys, .77 for girls) and high validity. The validity is demonstrated in part  by data showing that adolescents with various kinds of mental health disturbance have a significantly poorer self-image than adolescents who do not (Ebata and others, 1984).

**Results**

A repeated-measures multivariate analysis of variance was performed to determine whether the scores varied by sex or cohort and to examine the nature of developmental patterns over the three years studied. One possible set of developmental patterns consists of steady increases, steady decreases, or no change over time; this set of patterns was tested by fitting a straight line (linear polynomial) to the data. Another possible set of developmental patterns is curvilinear, with a dip or hump that we tested by fitting a curved line (quadratic polynomial) to the data.

The analysis revealed significant sex differences. As Figure 1 makes clear, boys generally reported higher average self-image scores than girls did over the three years studied. This is true for Emotional Tone, Body Image, Social Relationships, Mastery of the External World, (Less) Psychopathology, and Superior Adjustment, although boys were significantly higher in statistical terms only for Body Image. Girls were higher on Impulse Control, Family Relations, and Vocational-Educational Goals, which suggests that girls are better adjusted than boys are at home and at school and that they have less trouble than boys do in handling impulses.

There were significant multivariate effects for both the linear and the quadratic patterns, which indicates that self-image changes with age and that the rate of change is not uniform over the three years studied. The two sexes were not significantly different in the way in which self-image changed over time. Thus, although their mean level can be different, boys and girls develop in a basically parallel fashion over the early-adolescent years. However, both the linear and quadratic cohort-by-age interaction effects were significant. This indicates that the two cohorts followed different developmental paths. Examination of the cohort differences revealed that just two scales—Body Image and Social Relations—exhibited significantly different patterns by cohort and that in both cases the two cohorts differed not in direction of change over time but in magnitude of change. Thus, we felt that it was appropriate to combine cohorts in subsequent analyses and discussion.

Figure 1. Scale Means for Boys and Girls by Grade

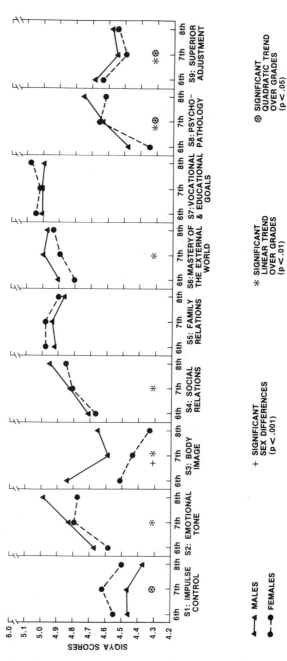

Figure 1 also illustrates the nature of self-image development over time. There is a linear increase in self-image in Emotional Tone, Social Relations, Mastery of the External World, and (Less) Psychopathology and a linear decrease in Body Image and Superior Adjustment. Impulse Control is curvilinear; it peaks in seventh grade. Family Relations and Vocational-Educational Goals do not change over time. The significant quadratic effect suggests a differential rate of change; for both increasing and decreasing scales, there is more change between sixth and seventh grades than between seventh and eighth grades (Abramowitz and others, 1984). Thus, early-adolescent self-image develops in a complex manner, with five dimensions rising, two remaining stable, and two declining.

## Discussion

How can these findings be interpreted in light of previous studies which showed that self-esteem dropped over this period? Simmons and colleagues (Simmons and others, 1973; Simmons and others, 1979; Blyth and others, 1983) reached findings which strongly suggest that self-esteem increases each year for boys in either setting and for girls who remain in an elementary school setting through eighth grade. Girls who move to a junior high setting are most at risk for disturbance in self-esteem and related self-measures.

In our study, as in Simmons's work (Rosenberg and Simmons, 1975; Simmons and Rosenberg, 1975), girls were generally lower in self-image through early adolescence. Yet, in our study the school transition did not seem to be a major source of distress; most self-image scales were higher for subjects who entered junior high school in seventh grade than they had been in the previous year. The two scales that decreased, Body Image and Superior Adjustment, both involve a high degree of social comparison. The Body Image scale taps satisfaction with appearance and physical development, and being the youngest students in a new school is likely to stimulate a decline in physical self-image. The Superior Adjustment scale assesses subjects' sense of themselves as excelling in the eyes of significant others and themselves; this sense is also likely to diminish in a new and challenging environment. Thus, our findings offer a more differentiated account of self-image change in early adolescence. The movement is generally positive, although there is a drop in two scales that emphasize social comparison.

## Conclusions

There has been much speculation about the mental health and self-image of young adolescents, the group thought to be at highest risk for adolescent turmoil. Our study fails to support the proposal that young people are generally tumultuous at this age. The reports of self-image in our data are generally positive, and they increase over the years studied. Of course, our data cannot tell us whether the same children held more positive self-perceptions in the past. In light of data from other studies, we assume that the positiveness of their self-views will increase steadily after the years of early adolescence.

We found that the self-views of girls were more negative than the self-views of boys. This is consistent with research on older adolescents and on adults (Gove and Herb, 1974; Offer and Howard, 1972). This sex difference seems to be related to the sex difference observed for the incidence of depression, which also seems to emerge during early adolescence (Petersen and Craighead, in press). A major component of the sex difference is body image. One would think that this aspect of self decreases in salience as one gets older. Yet, physical attractiveness remains more salient for women than it does for men (Lerner and Karabenick, 1974). It is important to emphasize, however, that sex differences were not found in the pattern of change over time, only in the level (positiveness) of self-image.

A major contribution of the research reported here — indeed of all research using the Offer Self-Image Questionnaire — is the specificity of results that measurement of multiple aspects of self-image affords. Patterns of change are different for different scales. The only changing scales that did not show a general upward movement were Impulse Control (which peaked at seventh grade), Body Image (which steadily declined), and Superior Adjustment (which dipped at seventh grade). These results seem to be both interrelated and consistent if we can speculate that the various components of Superior Adjustment were threatened by what was for most of the children in our sample a major school change at seventh grade. This change could trigger a sort of hyperreaction to control impulses as a way of coping. In the meantime, body image could continue to decline because of the changes that accompany puberty.

We do not want to leave the impression that early adolescence is an easy period of life that most young people sail through. On the contrary, there is a great deal of evidence that early adolescence is one of the most difficult phases of the life span (Petersen and Spiga, 1982). Thus, these data highlight the tremendous resilience and coping capacity that most young people can marshal to deal with the stressors of early adolescence.

## References

Abramowitz, R. H., and Asp, C. A. *The Ecology of Adolescence.* Unpublished manuscript, 1983.

Abramowitz, R. H., Schulenberg, J. E., Petersen, A. C., and Offer, D. "Developmental Change in Self-Image During Early Adolescence." Unpublished manuscript, 1984.

Baltes, P. B. "Longitudinal and Cross Sectional Sequences in the Study of Age and Generation Effects." *Human Development,* 1968, *11,* 145–171.

Blos, P. *On Adolescence: A Psychoanalytic Interpretation.* New York: Free Press, 1962.

Blyth, D. A., Simmons, R. G., and Carlton-Ford, S. "The Adjustment of Early Adolescents to School Transitions." *Journal of Early Adolescence,* 1983, *3,* 105–120.

Coleman, J. C. "Current Contradictions in Adolescent Theory." *Journal of Youth and Adolescence,* 1978, *3,* 105–120.

Conger, J. J., and Petersen, A. C. *Adolescence and Youth: Psychological Development in a Changing World.* (3rd ed.) New York: Harper & Row, 1984.

Coombs, A. W. "Some Observations on Self-Concept Theory and Research." In M. D. Lynch, A. A. Norem-Hebeisen, and K. J. Gergen (Eds.), *Self Concept: Advances in Theory and Research.* Cambridge, Mass.: Ballinger, 1981.

Deutsch, H. *Selected Problems of Adolescence.* New York: International Universities Press, 1967.

Douvan, E., and Adelson, J. *The Adolescent Experience.* New York: Wiley, 1966.

Dusek, J. B., and Flaherty, J. F. "The Development of Self-Concept During the Adolescent Years." *Monographs of the Society for Research in Child Development,* 1981, *46,* 1-67.

Ebata, A., Petersen, A. C., and Abramowitz, R. H. "Reports of Significant Psychopathology as Related to Psychosocial Development During Early Adolescence." Unpublished manuscript, 1984.

Freud, A. "Adolescence." *Psychoanalytic Study of the Child,* 1958, *13,* 255-278.

Gecas, V. "The Self-Concept." *Annual Review of Sociology,* 1982, *88,* 1-33.

Gove, W. R., and Herb, T. R. "Stress and Mental Illness Among the Young: A Comparison of the Sexes." *Social Forces,* 1974, *53,* 256-265.

Hall, G. S. *Adolescence.* New York: Appleton, 1904.

Hamburg, B. "Early Adolescence: A Specific and Stressful Stage of the Life Cycle." In G. V. Coelho, D. A. Hamburg, and J. E. Adams (Eds.), *Coping and Adaptation.* New York: Basic Books, 1974.

Inhelder, B., and Piaget, J. *The Growth of Logical Thinking: From Childhood to Adolescence.* New York: Basic Books, 1958.

Jorgenson, E. C., and Howell, J. R. "Changes in Self, Ideal-Self Correlations from Ages 8-18." *Journal of Social Psychology,* 1969, *68,* 63-67.

Kaplan, H. B. "The Self-Esteem Motive and Change in Self-Attitudes." *Journal of Nervous and Mental Disease,* 1975, *161,* 265-275.

Katz, P., and Zigler, E. "Self-Image Disparity: A Developmental Approach." *Journal of Personality and Social Psychology,* 1967, *5,* 186-195.

Kokenes, B. "Grade-Level Differences in Factors of Self-Esteem." *Developmental Psychology,* 1974, *10,* 954-958.

Lerner, R. M., and Karabenick, S. A. "Physical Attractiveness, Body Attitudes, and Self-Concept in Late Adolescents." *Journal of Youth and Adolescence,* 1974, *3,* 307-316.

McCarthy, J. D., and Hoge, D. R. "Analysis of Age Effects in Longitudinal Studies of Adolescent Self-Esteem." *Developmental Psychology,* 1982, *18,* 372-379.

Michael, W. B., Smith, R. A., and Michael, J. J. "The Factorial Validity of the Piers-Harris Children's Self-Concept Scale for Each of Three Samples of Elementary, Junior High, and High School Students in a Large Metropolitan School District." *Educational and Psychological Measurement,* 1975, *35,* 405-414.

Monge, R. H. "Developmental Trends in Factors of Adolescent Self-Concept." *Developmental Psychology,* 1973, *8,* 382-393.

Offer, D., and Howard, K. "An Empirical Analysis of the Offer Self-Image Questionnaire for Adolescents." *Archives of General Psychiatry,* 1972, *27,* 529-533.

Offer, D., and Offer, J. B. *From Teenage to Young Manhood.* New York: Basic Books, 1975.

Offer, D., Ostrov, E., and Howard, K. I. *The Adolescent: A Psychological Self-Portrait.* New York: Basic Books, 1981.

O'Malley, P. M., and Bachman, J. G. "Self-Esteem: Change and Stability Between Ages 13 and 23." *Developmental Psychology,* 1983, *19,* 257-268.

Petersen, A. C. "The Development of Self-Concept in Adolescence." In M. D. Lynch, A. A. Norem-Hebeisen, and K. J. Gergen (Eds.), *Self-Concept: Advances in Theory and Research.* Cambridge, Mass.: Ballinger, 1981.

Petersen, A. C. "Menarche: Meaning of Measures and Measuring Meaning." In S. Cobb (Ed.), *Menarche.* Lexington, Mass.: Heath, 1983a.

Petersen, A. C. "Pubertal Change and Cognition." In J. Brooks-Gunn and A. C. Petersen (Eds.), *Girls at Puberty: Biological and Psychosocial Perspectives.* New York: Plenum: 1983b.

Petersen, A. C., and Craighead, W. E. "Emotional and Personality Development in Normal Adolescents and Young Adults." In T. Millon and G. Klerman (Eds.), *Contemporary Issues in Psychotherapy.* New York: Guilford Press, in press.

Petersen, A. C., and Spiga, R. "Adolescence and Stress." In L. Goldberger and S. Breznitz (Eds.), *Handbook of Stress: Theoretical and Clinical Aspects.* New York: Macmillan, 1982.

Petersen, A. C., Tobin-Richards, M. H., and Boxer, A. M. "Puberty: Its Measurement and Its Meaning." *Journal of Early Adolescence,* 1983, *3,* 47-63.

Piers, E. V., and Harris, D. "Age and Other Correlates and Self-Concept in Children." *Journal of Educational Psychology,* 1964, *55,* 91-95.

Rosenberg, F. R., and Simmons, R. G. "Sex Differences in the Self-Concept of Adolescence." *Sex Roles,* 1975, *1,* 147-159.

Rosenberg, M. *Society and the Adolescent Self-Image.* Princeton, N.J.: Princeton University Press, 1965.

Rosenberg, M. *Conceiving the Self.* New York: Basic Books, 1979.

Rutter, M., Graham, P., Chadwick, O., and Yule, W. "Adolescent Turmoil: Fact or Fiction." *Journal of Child Psychology and Psychiatry,* 1976, *17,* 35-56.

Schaie, K. W. "A General Model for the Study of Developmental Problems." *Psychological Bulletin,* 1965, *64,* 92-107.

Schulenberg, J. E., Petersen, A. C., Abramowitz, R. H., and Offer, D. "A Self-Image Questionnaire for Young Adolescents (SIQYA)." *Journal of Youth and Adolescence,* 1984 (in press).

Sherwood, J. J. "Self-Identity and Referent Others." *Sociometry,* 1965, *28,* 66-81.

Simmons, R. G., Blyth, D. A., Van Cleave, E. F., and Bush, R. M. "Entry into Early Adolescence: The Impact of School Structure, Puberty, and Early Dating." *American Sociological Review,* 1979, *44,* 948-967.

Simmons, R. G., and Rosenberg, F. "Sex, Sex Roles, and Self-Image." *Journal of Youth and Adolescence,* 1975, *4,* 229-258.

Simmons, R. G., Rosenberg, F., and Rosenberg, M. "Disturbance in the Self-Image at Adolescence." *American Sociological Review,* 1973, *38,* 553-568.

Tobin-Richards, M., Boxer, A. M., and Petersen, A. C. "The Psychological Significance of Pubertal Change: Sex Differences in Perceptions of Self During Early Adolescence." In J. Brooks-Gunn and A. C. Petersen (Eds.), *Girls at Puberty: Biological and Psychosocial Perspectives.* New York: Plenum, 1983.

*Robert H. Abramowitz is a doctoral student in the Department of Human Development and Family Studies at Pennsylvania State University.*

*Anne C. Petersen is professor of Human Development and head of the Department of Individual and Family Studies at Pennsylvania State University.*

*John E. Schulenberg is a doctoral student in the Department of Human Development and Family Studies at Pennsylvania State University.*

*Mental health professionals view normal adolescents as being much more disturbed than they actually are.*

# The Mental Health Professional and the Normal Adolescent

*Shirley Hartlage*
*Kenneth I. Howard*
*Eric Ostrov*

This chapter presents evidence on the way in which mental health professionals view normal adolescents. The professional's concept of normal behavior influences every phase of practice, including diagnosis, treatment, and placement decision making. Yet, few empirical studies have directly assessed clinicians' perceptions of normal functioning, and only one study to date (Offer and others, 1981) has addressed the practitioner's views of normal adolescence. The purpose of this chapter is to extend previous reserach on mental health professional's knowledge of normal adolescents.

## Review of the Literature

Offer and Sabshin (1984) stress that there is little empirical base for conceptions of normal behavior, despite the vast clinical interest in and investigation of this topic. Offer and Sabshin define four perspectives on normality

The study described in this chapter was supported in part by the Adolescent Research Fund of the Department of Psychiatry at Michael Reese Hospital. The authors are grateful to Daniel Offer and Jennifer Crocker for their help in writing this chapter, and they thank the many professionals who participated in the study.

D. Offer, E. Ostrov, K. I. Howard (Eds.). *Patterns of Adolescent Self-Image.* New Directions for Mental Health Services, no. 22. San Francisco: Jossey-Bass, June 1984.

that can be found in the literature. The normality as health perspective encompasses the traditional medical-psychiatric approach. Normality is considered tantamount to health, and behavior is assumed to be normal when no manifest psychopathology is present. From this perspective, the term *health* refers to reasonable rather than to optimal functioning. The normality as utopia approach is either explicitly or implicitly embraced by psychoanalysts. This perspective conceives of normality as ideal functioning or self-actualization. The third perspective, normality as transactional systems, stresses the fact that definitions of what is normal change within individuals and throughout history over time. Normal behavior is viewed as the end result of interacting systems. Finally, the normality as average approach views normal functioning in terms of a statistically average range of behavior. Extremes are considered deviant. This chapter focuses on a study conducted from the normality as average perspective.

Two bodies of empirical research have a bearing on questions about the practitioner's view of normal functioning. The first group of studies asks clinicians to state their concepts of normal functioning and to agree or disagree with stated concepts. The second group of studies seeks to determine the accuracy of professionals' conceptualization of normal behavior.

In a national survey conducted by Goldman and Mendelsohn (1969), psychotherapists checked adjectives to describe an adult male who had satisfactory adaptation to himself and his environment. The representative sample, consisting of pyschiatric social workers, psychologists, and psychiatrists in approximately equal numbers, used Gough's Adjective Check List. The authors point out that this list uses no special language; it is free of psychiatric and theoretical terminology, it is not oriented toward pathology, and it is consistent with everyday ways of describing people. The authors found that when this theoretically neutral language was used, there was a marked consensus among therapists' descriptions of the normal male. Moreover, the normal adult male was described in very positive terms. Twenty-one adjectives were checked by more than 75 percent of the respondents: *adaptable* (94 percent), *dependable* (90 percent), *capable* (87 percent), *confident* (86 percent), *alert* (83 percent), *cooperative* (83 percent), *reasonable* (83 percent), *responsible* (83 percent), *active* (82 percent), *considerate* (81 percent), *mature* (80 percent), *sincere* (79 percent), *tolerant* (79 percent), *affectionate* (78 percent), *appreciative* (78 percent), *reliable* (78 percent), *self-confident* (78 percent), *warm* (78 percent), *conscientious* (77 percent), *stable* (76 percent), and *tactful* (76 percent). Respondents agreed that realistic orientation, social effectiveness, self-acceptance, freedom from inner conflict, and concern for the welfare of others were characteristic of normal adult men.

In a study of forty-six psychologists and psychologists in training that used a Q-set technique, Poe and Johnson (1972) found that respondents associated similar characteristics—dependability, responsibility, ethical behavior, and effectiveness in work and social relations—with optimal adjustment for the adult female. Subjects were instructed to describe a possible, rather than the ideal, level of effective functioning. Despite the presumable differences in respondents' theoretical orientations, there was significant agreement in their descriptions of optimal adjustment.

Thus, there appears to be a high degree of consensus among practitioners about some of the ascribed attributes of the normal individual. At the very least, professionals seem to concur that effectiveness in work and social relationships, concern for the welfare of others, and maturity are characteristic of normal adults. Such persons are consistently described as dependable, responsible, considerate, warm, and stable.

But, just how accurate are professionals' conceptions of the normal person? Studies comparing practitioners' perceptions of normal behavior with objective criteria constitute the second body of empirical research on clinicians' views of normal functioning.

Cline (1955) filmed supposed job interviews of male college students between the ages of eighteen and thirty-nine. These interviews consisted of a standard employment interview, a stress session in which the interviewer's questioning became critical and hostile, and an abreaction session in which the interviewer revealed the true nature of the interview and became quite deferential. A sequence of four such interviews was shown to various groups of professionals, students, and lay people. Subjects were asked to make behavioral predictions regarding the persons interviewed as well as to predict the interviewees' responses to the Personality Word Card. The Personality Word Card asked interviewees to select the adjectives that best described them from a group of 200 words. Cline found that the professional group, consisting of clinical psychologists, psychiatrists, and graduate clinical trainees, was more accurate than college students and other respondents who were not in the psychiatric professions. Within the professional group, increased length of experience was correlated with greater accuracy in predicting verbal behavior, but it was inversely related to facility in predicting real-life social behavior. Cline reported that having an accurate stereotype of the typical college male was helpful in predicting social and verbal behavior.

Other studies of the professional's accuracy in describing normal behavior have not been as favorable as Cline's. Benlifer and Kiesler (1972) studied twenty-five therapists and a matched group of adult laypersons. These researchers showed films of two preschool boys—one was severely disturbed, and the other was an unusually bright, well-adjusted child—to their subjects. Therapists made proportionally more maladjustment assertions, attributed more disturbance in psychiatric terms, and checked a greater number of psychiatric disorders for the normal child than the laypersons did. Next the researchers tested a sample of undergraduate freshmen who were completing a year-long introductory psychology course and who intended to major in psychology in order to ascertain whether the study of psychology attuned one to maladjustment. There were no differences between the responses of students and laypersons. However, the students' responses were closer to those of the therapists than to those of the laypersons in describing maladjustment in the normal child.

Offer and others (1981) studied sixty-two professionals who worked in a moderately sized psychiatric facility and a group of graduate students in psychology. Subjects were asked to predict the responses of mentally healthy adolescents to the Offer Self-Image Questionnaire. Results were compared with the response patterns of normal, emotionally disturbed, and delinquent youth. These authors found that mental health professionals viewed the normal adolescent as being significantly more disturbed in seven out of ten areas than the adolescents viewed themselves to be. In fact, mental health professionals conceptualized normal teenagers as stating that they had more problems than either the emotionally disturbed or the delinquent adolescents actually did. Graduate students in psychology also believed normal teens to be more maladusted than the teenagers saw themselves to be. However, graduate students did not perceive as much abnormal behavior as the practitioners did.

Thus, in different contexts, mental health professionals have shown various degrees of difficulty in predicting the behavior of normal individuals. All studies have shown some inaccuracies on the part of practitioners. Evidence on the mental health professional's views of normal functioning is scant and conflicting to some degree. Data are needed to clarify previous findings and to identify specific ways in which mental health professional's views are accurate or inaccurate.

## Method

*Subjects.* Hospital administrators of six adolescent psychiatric programs in a large metropolitan area were contacted in order to ascertain procedures and obtain approval for conducting research with therapeutic team members. Permission to carry out the study with staff members who were willing to participate was received from five administrators. The sixth agreed in principle; however, previous research commitments prevented implementation of the project in time to be reported here.

The senior author attended regularly scheduled team meetings, usually during the afternoon change of shifts. Personnel were told that research was being conducted in order to learn about mental health professionals' views of normal adolescents. Participation was voluntary. Staff members were offered individuals and group feedback in the form of confidential written score reports that they could compare with the responses of normal adolescents to learn in which areas their perceptions were accurate and in which areas they might misperceive the typical teenager. The vast majority of potential subjects were cooperative and enthusiastic about the prospect of feedback. Eighty-eight individuals participated. Participants included five psychiatrists, seven psychologists and psychology interns, nine social workers, sixteen nurses and nursing assistants, eleven mental health counselors and workers, eight psychiatric aides, nine teachers, including a school administrator, fifteen activities therapists, and three administrators. Five subjects did not list a profession.

*Procedures.* Subjects were asked to complete the Offer Self-Image Questionnaire (OSIQ) as they believed that a mentally healthy, well-adjusted adolescent of their sex would complete it. Respondents were randomly assigned to one of two age ranges—younger (thirteen- through fifteen-year-olds) or older (sixteen- through eighteen-year-olds). Anonymity was assured. The researcher generally remained until subjects had completed the questionnaire.

### Results

A comparison was made of the eleven scales for professionals ($N = 88$) with the eleven scales for professionals obtained by Offer, and others (1981) ($N = 58$) using a one-way multivariate analysis of variance. The resulting $F$, 1.38, was not significant. Professionals' perceptions of the typical teenager have been consistent over a period of years. These perceptions have been held by professionals who see hospitalized adolescents on a day-to-day basis as well as by those who have contact with disturbed youth in outpatient settings.

In view of this finding and in order to increase the reliability of percent endorsement interpretations, the two professional groups were combined for subsequent analyses. Of the total sample ($N = 146$), 24 professionals predicted the responses of younger males, 26 predicted the responses of older males, 49 predicted the responses of younger females, and 47 predicted the responses of older females.

Table 1 presents the average standard scores and, in parentheses, the standard deviations for the groups studied. Scores of less than 50 for the professionals signify a tendency to predict that normal adolescents report themselves to be more poorly adjusted than the adolescents themselves state. A difference of three points or more for professionals from the normal reference group is always statistically significant. A difference of at least five points is considered noteworthy.

Professionals view the typical teenager as being significantly more disturbed than the young people themselves report. Further, practitioners conceive of normal adolescents as being more poorly adjusted in five of ten areas than depressed teens or teens with conduct disorders themselves state (see Chapter Five).

Tables 2 through 6 show the percent endorsement of items by professionals and by adolescents in the normative sample. The "Describes me very well," "Describes me well," or "Describes me fairly well" responses constituted an endorsement. Only the items for which professionals either overestimated or underestimated the responses of all four normal adolescent groups— younger males, older males, younger females, and older females—by at least five percentage points have been included. Questions are grouped into the five self clusters (see Chapter One) as follows: Table 2 tabulates responses bearing on the psychological self, Table 3 tabulates responses bearing on the social self, Table 4 tabulates responses bearing on the sexual self, Table 5 tabulates responses bearing on the familial self, and Table 6 tabulates responses bearing

## Table 1. Offer Self-Image Questionnaire Standard Scores Comparing Groups Studied

| Self and Scale | Professionals (N = 146) | Depressed[a] (N = 213) | Conduct[a] Disorders (N = 68) |
|---|---|---|---|
| **Psychological Self** | | | |
| I. Impulse control | 46 (14) | 45 (16) | 45 (18) |
| II. Emotional tone | 43 (17) | 44 (17) | 43 (16) |
| III. Body and self-image | 45 (15) | 49 (17) | 50 (18) |
| **Social Self** | | | |
| IV. Social relationships | 41 (15) | 48 (17) | 47 (20) |
| V. Morals | 50 (16) | 44 (16) | 42 (15) |
| IX. Vocational and educational goals | 42 (15) | 49 (17) | 45 (19) |
| **Sexual Self** | | | |
| VI. Sexual attitudes | 44 (13) | 51 (16) | 52 (18) |
| **Familial Self** | | | |
| VII. Family relationships | 41 (14) | 40 (16) | 28 (19) |
| **Coping Self** | | | |
| VIII. Mastery of external world | 44 (17) | 45 (18) | 46 (19) |
| X. Psychopathology | 46 (15) | 46 (17) | 46 (19) |
| XI. Superior adjustment | 48 (14) | 48 (17) | 44 (18) |

*Note:* Scores presented are average standard scores and, in parentheses, standard deviations.
[a]This sample is described in Chapter Five.

on the coping self. Within each table, items are ordered from those for which professionals' responses indicate the greatest underestimate of adolescent self-image to those for which the professionals' responses indicate the greatest over-estimate.

The criterion that professionals would underestimate the self-image of normal adolescents by at least five percentage points in all four age and sex categories was met on twenty-six items, while professionals consistently over-estimated the percent endorsement of the typical adolescent on eleven items. This means that practitioners misperceived the responses of normal teenagers on 28 percent of the 130 items.

The misconceptions that mental health professionals hold about the normal adolescent form clear and consistent patterns. In the area of the psychological self (Table 2), professionals made relatively accurate predictions on the Impulse Control and Body and Self-Image scales. However, they expected typical teenagers to be more poorly adjusted in the area of Emotional Tone than teens themselves reported. Similarly, the Emotional Tone of depressed adolescents and of adolescents with conduct disorders differs markedly from that of normals (see Chapter Five).

With regard to emotions, professionals perceived normal adolescents

## Table 2. Psychological Self: Average Percent Endorsement
## of Items by Adolescents and Professionals

| Item | Mental Health Professionals | Normal Adolescents |
|---|---|---|
| I.34. "I can take criticism without resentment." | 32 | 58 |
| II.38. "My feelings are easily hurt." | 76 | 50 |
| I.59. "Even under pressure I manage to remain calm." | 54 | 70 |
| II.44. "I feel relaxed under normal circumstances." | 78 | 91 |
| I.81. "I fear something constantly." | 12 | 26 |
| II.54. "I am so very anxious." | 25 | 53 |

*Note:* Entries above the horizontal line are items on which mental health professionals overestimated normal adolescent psychopathology. Entries below the line are items on which they underestimated psychopathology.

as being more defensive, more sensitive, and more tense under normal circumstances than the young people described themselves as being. Professionals believed that teens are more resentful of criticism and that their feelings are more easily hurt than the young people themselves reported. Practitioners viewed teenagers as being less relaxed both under usual circumstances and under pressure than normal adolescents stated.

While professionals overestimated the emotionality of adolescents under normal circumstances, including pressure situations, they underestimated the number of normal adolescents who experienced extremes of emotion. More normal teenagers than professionals expected said that they feared something "constantly" and that they were "very anxious."

In the area of the social self (Table 3), practitioners expected typical adolescents to see themselves as more poorly adjusted with regard to social relationships and vocational and educational goals than was actually the case. However, they made accurate predictions with regard to normal young people on the morals scale.

The theme of adolescents' perceived defensiveness and sensitivity is prominent in the professionals' perception of teenagers' interpersonal relationships. Practitioners thought that teens were more apt to mind being corrected and to become upset if others disapproved of them than the teenagers reported being. Professionals also expected adolescents to blame others even when they knew that they were at fault more frequently than the teens themselves reported.

Professionals thought that teenagers were more socially ill at ease than the young people believed. However, their responses to other items (for example, "I enjoy most parties I go to") indicate that practitioners recognized that the great majority of teens do enjoy the company of others. Professionals tended to believe that adolescents place more emphasis on peer relationships than

## Table 3. Social Self: Average Percent Endorsement of
## Items by Adolescents and Professionals

| Item | Mental Health Professionals | Normal Adolescents |
|---|---|---|
| IV.65. "I do not mind being corrected since I can learn from it." | 47 | 80 |
| IV.86. "If others disapprove of me I get terribly upset." | 61 | 39 |
| V.40. "I blame others even when I know I was at fault." | 52 | 32 |
| IX.37. "I am sure that I will be proud of my future profession." | 69 | 86 |
| IV.13. "I usually feel out of place at picnics or parties." | 29 | 23 |
| IV.75. "I prefer being alone than with people my own age." | 8 | 22 |
| V.120. "I would not like to be associated with kids who 'hit below the belt.'" | 88 | 66 |

*Note:* Entries above the horizontal line are items on which mental health professionals overestimated normal adolescent psychopathology. Entries below the line are items on which they underestimated psychopathology.

teens themselves stated, and they viewed teenagers as less apt to prefer being alone than the adolescents themselves reported.

In the area of vocational and educational goals, mental health professionals underestimated the pride that adolescents expected to feel about their future professions. This is only one of several instances in which practitioners tended to perceive adolescents as being less confident about their ability to cope than the teenagers themselves believed.

The professionals' concept of normal adolescent morality is more accurate than their concepts in any other area. Professionals rarely underestimated the adjustment of normals with regard to moral issues. In fact, professionals overestimated normal teens' unwillingness to associate with kids who "hit below the belt."

Professionals conceived of normal teenagers as being far more confused about their sexual attitudes than the teens perceived themselves to be (Table 4). Forty percent more of the professionals than of the adolescents endorsed the item "It is very hard for a teenager to know how to handle sex in a right way." Even allowing for some braggadocio and defensiveness on the part of the teens, real misconceptions appear to exist in this area. Teenagers are viewed both as thinking about sex more frequently than they do and as being more frightened by it than it appears that they are. Professionals think that teenagers are more insecure with regard to their sexuality — for example,

## Table 4. Sexual Self: Average Percent Endorsement of
## Items by Adolescents and Professionals

| Item | Mental Health Professionals | Normal Adolescents |
|------|------|------|
| VI.16. "It is very hard for a teenager to know how to handle sex in a right way." | 67 | 27 |
| VI.91. "Sexually I am way behind." | 43 | 21 |
| VI.10. "The opposite sex finds me a bore." | 33 | 13 |
| VI.97. "Thinking or talking about sex frightens me." | 22 | 9 |
| VI.28. "Dirty jokes are fun at times." | 94 | 77 |
| VI.119. "Having a girlfriend/boyfriend is important to me." | 91 | 74 |
| VI.122. "I often think about sex." | 90 | 68 |

*Note:* Entries above the horizontal line are items on which mental health professionals overestimated normal adolescent psychopathology. Entries below the line are items on which they underestimated psychopathology.

that they more often see themselves as sexually behind and more often believe that the opposite sex finds them a bore — than the teenagers report themselves to be. Practitioners continue to place undue emphasis on the value of peer relationships to teens when they overestimate the importance to teenagers of having a boyfriend or girlfriend.

The area in which professionals encountered the greatest difficulty in predicting the reponses of normal adolescents, the familial self (Table 5), is the area in which the responses of both depressed teens and teens with conduct disorders differed most from those of the typical young person (see Chapter Five). Professionals misperceived adolescents' feelings about their parents and their views of their parents' treatment of them. Contrary to what the majority of professionals thought, four fifths of our normal adolescent respondents indicated that they understood their parents to some extent, and only about 30 percent favored one parent much more than the other. The responses of normal adolescents depicted fair treatment by parents. In contrast, professionals expected adolescents to say that their parents played favorites. The great majority of teens thought that their parents were patient, and most also thought that their parents were right when they were strict. Few professionals expected them to say this.

While professionals misconstrued adolescents' feelings about their parents, they were more accurate in predicting adolescent perceptions of parents' feelings toward them. Discrepancies between adolescents' and professionals' endorsement of items indicative of parental satisfaction with and pride in their child were small.

## Table 5. Familial Self: Average Percent Endorsement of Items by Adolescents and Professionals

| Item | Mental Health Professionals | Normal Adolescents |
|---|---|---|
| VII.24. "Understanding my parents is beyond me." | 53 | 19 |
| VII.87. "I like one parent much better than the other." | 52 | 28 |
| VII.9. "My parents are almost always on the side of someone else, for example, my brother or sister." | 52 | 32 |
| VII.71. "My parents are usually patient with me." | 63 | 80 |
| VII.55. "When my parents are strict, I feel that they are right even if I get angry." | 56 | 39 |

## Table 6. Coping Self: Average Percent Endorsement of Items by Adolescents and Professionals

| Item | Mental Health Professionals | Normal Adolescents |
|---|---|---|
| X.2. "I am afraid that someone is going to make fun of me." | 62 | 23 |
| XI.49. "Our society is a competitive one, and I am not afraid of it." | 43 | 68 |
| X.29. "I often blame myself even when I'm not really at fault." | 58 | 40 |
| X.31. "The size of my sex organs is normal." | 77 | 93 |
| X.36. "Sometimes I feel so ashamed of myself that I just want to hide in a corner and cry." | 42 | 26 |
| XI.11. "If I would be separated from all people I know, I feel that I would not be able to make a go of it." | 49 | 33 |
| X.126. "I do not have any fears which I cannot understand." | 57 | 71 |
| X.127. "No one can harm me just by not liking me." | 58 | 69 |
| X.45. "I feel empty emotionally most of the time." | 13 | 20 |
| X.111. "When I am with people I am bothered by hearing strange noises." | 5 | 14 |
| X.96. "I believe I can tell the real from the fantastic." | 92 | 82 |
| XI.56. "Working closely with another fellow never gives me pleasure." | 4 | 29 |

*Note:* Entries above the horizontal line are items on which mental health professionals overestimated normal adolescent psychopathology. Entries below the line are items on which they underestimated psychopathology.

In the area of the coping self (Table 6), mental health professionals made relatively accurate predictions about the reactions of normal adolescents on the Superior Adjustment and Psychopathology scales. However, they expected normal teenagers to report themselves to be more poorly adjusted on the Mastery of the External World scale than the teenagers themselves did.

The picture held by professionals of the normal adolescent's ability to cope contrasts sharply with that of the adolescents themselves. Professionals believed that teens were more fearful of being made fun of and of societal competition than the teens reported themselves as being. Practitioners also thought that teenagers had more fears that they did not understand.

Mental health professionals thought that teenagers experienced more undue guilt than the typical adolescent stated. They incorrectly reported that the majority of adolescents often blamed themselves, even when they were not at fault. They were also more likely to expect a teen to feel so ashamed that he or she wanted to hide in a corner and cry.

Many of the misconceptions held by professionals can be summarized by their underendorsement of the item "I feel empty emotionally most of the time." On the contrary, mental health professionals view normal adolescents as being full of emotion. They think that teenagers are more sensitive, more tense, more fearful, and more guilt-ridden than the teenagers perceive themselves to be.

Professional misconceptions about the importance of peer relationships to the normal teen seem to go even further in the area of coping. Here, adolescents are perceived not only as emphasizing peer relationships but as believing that they will not be able to make a go of it without the people they now know. About 33 percent of the normal adolescents in our study actually thought this, but 49 percent of the professionals endorsed the same item. Practitioners were also more apt to think that adolescents believed that they could be harmed by someone's not liking them. Consistently, professionals expected more teenagers to report gaining plesure from working closely with another than teenagers actually did.

Professionals underestimated the number of normal teens who experienced unusual psychiatric symptoms, such as hearing noises and inability to distinguish the real from the fantastic. In fact, their underestimation of adolescent adjustment on these items counterbalanced their overestimation of adjustment with regard to emotionality, resulting in an overall correct prediction in the area of psychopathology that may be somewhat misleading.

## Discussion

The pattern of misconceptions held by mental health professionals about normal adolescents is strongly convergent with the turmoil theory of adolescence, which was examined in Chapter One. The emphasis that professionals place on psychological disequilibrium is evidenced by their perceptions of teenagers as fearful, hypersensitive, and tense. They think that teenagers experience confusion about sexual matters and that teenagers' family experience confusion about sexual matters and that teenagers' family relationships are adversarial. In each of these aspects, the professionals' perceptions of normal adolescents resemble the self-descriptions of disturbed teenagers more closely than they do the self-descriptions of normal adolescents. Several lines of argument could account for this bias.

Cognitive social psychologists (Nisbett and Ross, 1980) point out that expectations and stereotypes lead to biased judgments through the encoding, storage, and retrieval stages of information processing. First, ambiguous instances are encoded in line with expectations (Sagar and Schofield, 1980), while disconfirming cases are explained away by situational causes (Bell and others, 1976; Crocker and others, 1983; Deaux and Emswiller, 1974; Hayden and Mischel, 1976; Kulik, 1983). Thus, if a practitioner encounters a normal adolescent who expresses positive feelings about his or her parents, the practitioner will tend to infer that the adolescent is simply in an unusually good mood.

Furthermore, when people are unable to recall information, they use their stereotypes to infer or guess what the information was (Belleza and Bower, 1981; Cohen, 1981). Thus, in trying to decide what normal adolescents are like, practitioners who expect them to be fearful but who are unable to recall instances of fearful adolescents may still affirm statements suggesting that this is the case.

Edwards (1968) reports that, when presented with new information, people adjust their opinions, but the adjustment is insufficient. Thus, if clinicians begin their practice with misconceptions about the typical adolescent, working with disturbed teenagers is likely to strengthen these misperceptions. Experience with normal teenagers may improve the accuracy of their perceptions, but it will not rid them of misconceptions.

Even without preconceived notions, practitioners have ample reason to misperceive normal adolescents. Tversky and Kahneman (1974) point out that people sometimes assess the probability of an event by the ease with which instances or occurrences of it can be brought to mind. It is far easier for professionals who work with disturbed adolescents to recall instances of maladjustment than it is for laypersons. Since the disturbed adolescents with whom professionals work show marked deficits in their family relationships, the professionals will have no difficulty in recalling such instances.

Further, extreme instances of behavior have a disproportionate influence on one's stereotypes (Rothbart and others, 1978). Visual salience (Tversky and Kahneman, 1974; Hamilton, 1979) and recency (Tversky and Kahneman, 1974) also affect the retrievability of instances. The extreme behaviors of disturbed teenagers are apt to be salient and recent for the practitioner who works with these adolescents on a day-to-day basis. It is also the case that imagining something increases its subjective probability (Carroll, 1978). It is likely that clinicians who work with disturbed teenagers frequently think about them and their behaviors, even when they are not in direct contact with these young people.

Predictive accuracy depends on one's ability to vary one's judgments as the situation varies and on one's ability to approximate the actual situation (Cronbach, 1955). Adolescents who exhibit abnormal behavior are more apt than normal adolescents to have been in aversive situations and to have dealt with them ineffectively. Thus, the practitioner who is frequently exposed to maladjustment may be led to overestimate both the number of difficult situations that teens encounter and the average way in which adolescents deal with such problems.

Moreover, training may increase the readiness of professionals to perceive abnormality. Results of studies by Benlifer and Kiesler (1972) and by Offer and others (1981) support this hypothesis. Soskin (1954) found that a group consisting of ten graduate students in clinical pyschology and two supervisors attributed more maladjustment to a stimulus person than a group of less experienced graduate students did. Similarly, in a study by Crow (1957), medical students lost accuracy in predicting the responses of patients on personality questionnaires as a result of training in interpersonal relations.

That differences in training and subsequent theoretical orientation yield differing degrees of readiness to perceive maladjustment has been demonstrated by Langer and Abelson (1974). Forty clinicians who were associated with universities representing two different schools of thought viewed a videotaped interview of a man who had recently applied for a new job. Half of each group was told that the interviewee was a job applicant, and half was told that he was a patient. Analytic therapists described the interviewee as significantly more disturbed when he was labeled patient, whereas behavior therapists described the man as fairly well adjusted regardless of the label supplied.

Training may have a direct effect on perception. Toch and Schulte (1961) tachistoscopically presented police administration students and novices with a violent picture to one eye and a matched neutral picture to the other. Trained subjects saw more violent pictures than controls did. Neisser (1967) points out that, because the quantity and variety of information available at any one time is greater than anyone can process or attend to, individuals must be selective in what they notice in any situation.

Whatever the reasons for practitioners' misconceptions, an accurate perception of normal adolescence is crucial to diagnosis, treatment, and placement decision making. Mental health professionals need to be aware of their general tendency to see pathology as well as of specific inaccuracies in their views. Training in the characteristics of normal teenagers is essential for the mental health professional, and this training needs to be based on empirical findings about normality, not on theoretical conjecture.

## References

Bell, L. G., Wicklund, R. A., Manko, G., and Larkin, C. "When Unexpected Behavior Is Attributed to the Environment." *Journal of Research in Personality*, 1976, *10*, 316–327.
Belleza, F. S., and Bower, G. H. "Person Stereotypes and Memory for People." *Journal of Personality and Social Psychology*, 1981, *41*, 856–865.

Benlifer, V. E., and Kiesler, S. B. "Psychotherapists' Perceptions of Adjustment and Attraction Toward Children Described as in Therapy." *Journal of Experimental Research in Personality*, 1972, *6* (2-3), 169-177.

Carroll, J. S. "Effect of Imagining an Event on Expectations for Event: Interpretation in Terms of Availability Heuristic." *Journal of Experimental Social Psychology*, 1978, *14*, 88-96.

Cline, V. B. "Ability to Judge Personality Assessed with a Stress Interview and Sound Film Technique." *Journal of Abnormal and Social Psychology*, 1955, *50*, 183-187.

Cohen, C. "Person Categories and Social Perception: Testing Some Boundaries of the Processing Effects of Prior Knowledge." *Journal of Personality and Social Psychology*, 1981, *40*, 441-452.

Crocker, J., Hannah, D. B., and Weber, R. "Person Memory and Causal Attributions." *Journal of Personality and Social Psychology*, 1983, *44*, 55-66.

Cronbach, L. J. "Processes Affecting Scores on 'Understanding of Others' and 'Assumed Similarity.'" *Psychological Bulletin*, 1955, *52*, 177-193.

Crow, W. J. "The Effect of Training upon Accuracy and Variability in Interpersonal Perception." *Journal of Abnormal and Social Psychology*, 1957, *55*, 355-359.

Deaux, K., and Emswiller, T. "Explanations for Successful Performance on Sex-Linked Tasks: What Is Skill for the Male Is Luck for the Female." *Journal of Personality and Social Psychology*, 1974, *29*, 80-85.

Edwards, W. "Conservatism in Human Information Processing." In B. Kleinmuntz (Ed.), *Formal Representation of Human Judgment*. New York: Wiley, 1968.

Goldman, R. K., and Mendelsohn, G. A. "Psychotherapeutic Change and Social Adjustment: A Report of a National Survey of Psychotherapists." *Journal of Abnormal Psychology*, 1969, *74*, 164-172.

Hamilton, D. L. "A Cognitive-Attributional Analysis of Stereotyping." In L. Berkowitz (Ed.), *Advances in Experimental Social Psychology*. Vol. 12. New York: Academic Press, 1979.

Hayden, T., and Mischel, W. "Maintaining Trait Consistency in the Resolution of Behavioral Inconsistency: The Wolf in Sheep's Clothing." *Journal of Personality*, 1976, *44*, 109-132.

Kulik, J. A. "Confirmatory Attribution and the Attribution of Social Beliefs." *Journal of Personality and Social Psychology*, 1983, *44*, 1171-1181.

Langer, E. J., and Abelson, R. P. "A Patient by Any Other Name . . . : Clinician Group Difference in Labeling Bias." *Journal of Consulting and Clinical Psychology*, 1974, *42*, 4-9.

Neisser, U. *Cognition and Reality: Principles and Implications of Social Psychology*. San Francisco: W. H. Freeman, 1967.

Nisbett, R., and Ross, L. *Human Inference: Strategies and Shortcomings of Social Judgment*. Englewood Cliffs, N.J.: Prentice-Hall, 1980.

Offer, D., Ostrov, E., and Howard, K. I. "The Mental Health Professional's Concept of the Normal Adolescent." *Archives of General Psychiatry*, 1981, *38*, 149-152.

Offer, D., and Sabshin, M. *Normality and the Life Cycle*. New York: Basic Books, 1984.

Poe, C. A., and Johnson, S. "Psychologists' Conception of Optimal Adjustment." *Journal of Clinical Psychology*, 1972, *28* (4), 449-451.

Rothbart, M., Fulero, S., Jensen, C., Howard, J., and Birrell, P. "From Individual to Group Impressions: Availability Heuristics in Stereotype Formation." *Journal of Experimental Social Psychology*, 1978, *14*, 237-255.

Sagar, H. A., and Schofield, J. W. "Racial and Behavioral Cues in Black and White Children's Perceptions of Ambiguously Aggressive Acts." *Journal of Personality and Social Psychology*, 1980, *39*, 590-598.

Soskin, W. F. "Bias in Postdiction from Projection Tests." *Journal of Abnormal and Social Psychology*, 1954, *49*, 69-74.

Toch, H. H., and Schulte, R. "Readiness to Perceive Violence as a Result of Police Training." *British Journal of Psychology*, 1961, *52*, 389-393.

Tversky, A., and Kahneman, D. "Judgment Under Uncertainty: Heuristics and Biases." *Science*, 1974, *185*, 1124–1131.

*Shirley Hartlage is a doctoral student in the Department of Psychology at Northwestern University. Former program facilitator for the Special Education District of Lake County, Illinois, she taught emotionally disturbed adolescents at Harding Hospital School in Worthington, Ohio.*

*Kenneth I. Howard is professor of psychology at Northwestern University; professor of psychology at Northwestern University Medical School; senior research consultant in the Department of Psychiatry at Michael Reese Hospital and Medical Center; and senior research consultant at the Institute for Juvenile Research.*

*Eric Ostrov is director of forensic psychology in the Department of Psychiatry at Michael Reese Hospital and Medical Center and research associate (assistant professor) in the Department of Psychiatry at the University of Chicago Pritzker School of Medicine.*

*Inpatient adolescents with different DSM-III diagnoses
display different patterns of depression.*

# Prominent Features of Depression in Affective- and Conduct-Disordered Inpatients

David J. Berndt
David Zinn

Three somewhat different viewpoints are evident in American psychiatry with
regard to the role of depression in children and adolescents. The perspective
with the longest history holds that depressive phenomena in young people generally are not part of a full depressive syndrome. While this perspective is less
popular today in America than it was in the past, it remains a common position, and most other countries advocate some variant of this viewpoint. For example, in his textbook on adolescent psychiatry, the British psychiatrist John
Evans (1982) devotes only one page to a discussion of "abnormal" depression
in adolescence and questions whether depression might be more appropriately
viewed as a secondary effect of other psychiatric problems than as a clinical en-
tity in itself. Similarly, a group of Australian researchers (Werry and others,
1983) diagnosed 195 inpatient youths with DSM-III criteria and found only
one with affective disorder, a bipolar adolescent. These authors suggest that,
at least in their research group, the kind of patient who received a diagnosis of
depression in America would be diagnosed as having adjustment disorder with
depressed mood.

The second perspective, which was particularly prominent in the late
1960s and early 1970s, maintains that certain behaviors, such as acting out,

D. Offer, E. Ostrov, K. I. Howard (Eds.). *Patterns of Adolescent Self-Image.* New Directions
for Mental Health Services, no. 22. San Francisco: Jossey-Bass, June 1984.

school failure avoidance, and running away, serve either to mask the depression (Glaser, 1967) or to express depressive equivalents (Lesse, 1974, Spiegel, 1974; Toolan, 1962). Kovacs and Beck (1977) catalogue and review the positions of several writers from this school.

Cytryn and McKnew (1974) originally advocated the masked depression approach. However, they recently (Cytryn and others, 1980) adopted a third point of view, which is more or less commonly accepted and which is reflected both in DSM-III and in a number of studies reported in Cantwell and Carlson (1983). Simply stated, this position holds that childhood and adolescent depression can be diagnosed reliably by using adult criteria and structured interviews with only minor modifications to account for the influence of development or maturational processes. Delinquency, acting out, and other features associated with conduct disorders are relegated to the role of distractors when they co-occur.

The research discussed in this chapter focused on depressive symptomatology in adolescent inpatients. In DMS-III, the criteria for the conduct disorder diagnostic group include many of the features believed to be depressive equivalents. By dividing patients into three groups — one with "pure" conduct disorder, one with depression (as defined by DSM-III), and one with both diagnoses — we endeavored to answer this question: For depressed inpatient adolescents whose only DSM-III diagnosis is depression, are the depressive symptom patterns and the severity of depressive symptoms comparable with those of other inpatient adolescents, especially of adolescents with pure conduct disorders and adolescents with symptoms of both conduct disorder and depression?

## Method

*Subjects.* Participants were forty-two consecutive consenting inpatient adolescents admitted to the psychiatric unit of a large, private urban hospital. They ranged in age from thirteen to eighteen years; the average was 16.2 years. Males comprised 43 percent of the subjects, while 57 percent were female. Most of the subjects were white and came from social classes II and III. Most patients were assessed within three weeks of admission. Exclusion criteria included patients with organic brain deficits. Three patients declined to participate in the study. Nearly all the patients were free of major tranquilizers when they were assessed, although a few were on antidepressants or minor tranquilizers.

*Diagnosis.* Patients were interviewed in the early part of their hospital stay by either one or two clinically experienced researchers, who used a modified Kiddie-SADS interview (Chambers and others, 1978). Where there were two interviewers, one was a psychiatrist, and one was a psychologist, or both were psychologists. For 38 percent of the subjects, there was only one interviewer. However, most of these interviews were audiotaped, and the taped interview was assessed by a second rater. Six subjects were administered a differently structured interview, which is still under development. Information from the Kiddie-SADS interview provided a standardized data base comparable to that used in other settings. Data from the interview and information from other sources such as chart material and family interviews were then summarized by one of the interviewers and presented to the research diagnostic team. The diagnostic team usually included both authors; it ranged in size from two to five members. The other members of the team were either psychiatrists or psychologists who had research experience.

Diagnosis was reached by consensus for all cases using DSM-III criteria and the data just outlined. Four different clusters of patients were selected for the purposes of the study. The pure conduct disorder group comprised eleven patients who met one of the four DSM-III sets of diagnostic criteria for conduct disorder and did not qualify for a diagnosis of depression. Other diagnoses, such as substance abuse, were not a focus of the research, and they are not reported here. The pure depression group included ten patients who met DSM-III criteria for atypical depression, dysthymic disorder, or major depressive episode (either unipolar or bipolar); these patients were not eligible for either conduct disorder or any other psychiatric diagnosis. Ten patients were identified as mixed because they qualified both for a depression diagnosis and for a conduct disorder diagnosis. No attempt was made to identify a primary diagnosis, since it had been our experience that any such designation could be made only by following arbitrary rules that have not been demonstrated to be either valid or clinically useful. The fourth group included four patients with anorexia nervosa, three patients with pervasive developmental disorder, and four patients with other diagnoses. Of the eleven patients in this "other" group, five also qualified for a second diagnosis of depression. Many patients in this group had two primary diagnoses, and one had three.

*Multiscore Depression Inventory.* Patients completed the Multiscore Depression Inventory (MDI) (Berndt and others, 1980) in the first weeks of their hospitalization, usually within one or two days of the diagnostic interview. The MDI was handscored by a researcher blind to the diagnosis.

The Multiscore Depression Inventory is a 118-item true-false self-report questionnaire that measures the severity of depression. It has ten reliable subscales for different depressive features or symptoms. Evidence demonstrates that the MDI has acceptable validity and reliability (Berndt, 1981; Berndt and Berndt, 1980; Berndt, Berndt, and Byars, 1983; Berndt and others, 1980; Stuckey, 1981) and that it is one of the more easily read self-report depression scales (Berndt, Schwartz, and Kaiser, 1983). It has often been used with adolescents (Berndt and others, 1982), and a short form (forty-seven items) has also proven useful (Berndt, Petzel, and Kaiser, 1983; Joy, 1981). Spanish- and French-language versions are currently being developed.

Normative data are available on more than 2,000 subjects. The MDI correlates highly with the Beck Depression Inventory (Beck, 1967), Lubin's Depression Adjective Checklist (Lubin, 1967), the Zung Self-Rating Depression Scale (Zung, 1965), and other self-report measures. The relationship between the MDI and personality inventories is described by Petzel and Berndt (1983).

The ten subscales of the MDI include several features of depression, including guilt, pessimism, irritability, low self-esteem, social introversion and withdrawal, sad mood, lack of energy (fatigability), cognitive difficulty, and two kinds of helplessness: instrumental and learned. Since the scales are face valid (Berndt and others, 1980), most of the names describe the subscales adequately. The three subscales that need further elaboration are cognitive difficulty, learned helplessness, and instrumental helplessness. Cognitive difficulty includes indecisiveness as well as slowed or muddled thinking.

The differences between learned helplessness and instrumental helplessness are discussed by Berndt (1981). Learned helplessness refers to a generalized belief that action and its consequences are noncontingent. Patients who score high on this scale report that they have no control over their lives and they do not see any point in trying. Anhedonia and lack of interest in the world are central motivational features of depression in Seligman's (1975) early model of learned helplessness, which provided the conceptual basis for this scale. Learned helplessness is a passive kind of helplessness, more likely to be related to either anaclitic or endogenous depression than to reactive depression.

In contrast to the passive stance measured by the learned helplessness scale, instrumental helplessness measures an active helplessness, in which the respondent either actively seeks help from others (often manipulatively) or at least greatly desires help from others. Consequently, the belief that others can help but are not doing enough is a central theme. Persons who score high on this scale are highly aware of reinforcement contingencies, especially those that are social. These persons believe that they are being slighted, that they are getting a raw deal out of life, and that they are in a state of social deprivation. Reactive depression, particularly in patients who have prominent narcissistic features or who process loss primarily as deprivation, is reflected by high scores on instrumental helplessness.

On the MDI, raw scores are converted into standardized scores in comparison to age- and sex-appropriate norms. The data are then expressed as in Figures 1 and 2, as standardized scores with a mean of fifty and a standard deviation of ten. High scores on the MDI and the ten subscales are interpreted as indicative of greater pyschopathology.

### Results

Figures 1 and 2 illustrate the pattern of depressive symptoms reported by the forty-two adolescent patients in our study on the MDI. As Figure 1 illustrates, depressed and mixed groups were clearly more symptomatic than the conduct-disordered patients, who were at or below the average compared to age-appropriate norms. Figure 2 compares the depressed and conduct-disordered patients with a group of other psychiatric patients. This "other"

## Figure 1. Comparison of Symptom Profiles of Conduct-Disordered, Depressed, and Mixed Diagnostic Groups

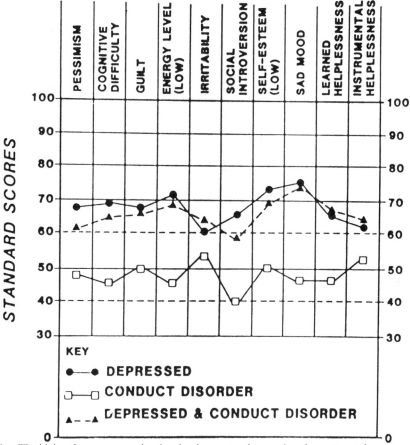

*Note:* The higher the score on each subscale, the greater the severity of symptomatology.

group, described earlier, includes five patients with an additional Axis I diagnosis of affective disorder; none of the patients had a second diagnosis of conduct disorder.

One-way analyses of variance were computed for raw scores on the MDI and its ten subscales, with diagnosis (depression, conduct-disordered, mixed, and other) as the independent variable. For the full-scale MDI, results indicate significant differences among the four groups ($F$ (3, 38) = 29.61, $p < .001$). A post hoc Scheffé analysis at the .05 criterion level indicated that subjects with conduct disorders were significantly less depressed ($M = 26.82$; SD = 10.83) than subjects in the depressed group ($M = 85.10$; SD = 14.55), subjects in the mixed group ($M = 80.00$; SD = 9.51), and subjects in the "other" group ($M = 51.45$; SD = 24.57). Subjects in the "other" group were also significantly less depressed than those in the mixed and depressed groups.

### Figure 2. Comparison of Symptom Profiles of Depressed, Conduct-Disordered, and Other Diagnostic Groups

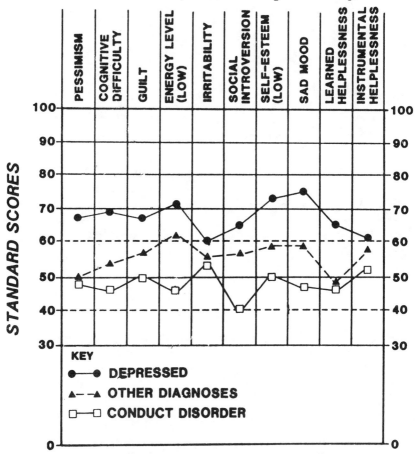

*Note:* The higher the score on each subscale, the greater the severity of symptomatology.

Similar results were noted for the subscales. Significant differences were noted for all ten MDI symptom subscales: sad mood ($F(3,38) = 15.86;$ $p < .001$), social introversion ($F(3,38) = 11.49;$ $p < .001$), self-esteem ($F(3,38) = 8.34;$ $p < .001$), irritability ($F(3,38) = 15.42;$ $p < .001$), cognitive difficulty ($F(3,38) = 4.06;$ $p < .05$), energy level ($F(3,38) = 15.10;$ $p < .001$), learned helplessness ($F(3,38) = 11.78;$ $p < .001$), instrumental helplessness ($F(3,38) = 24.27;$ $p < .001$), guilt $F(3,38) = 15.34;$ $p < .001$), and pessimism ($F(3,38) = 4.68;$ $p < .01$).

Post hoc Scheffé analyses with a .05 criterion generally indicated that subjects in the conduct-disordered group were less symptomatic than subjects in the other groups. Table 1, which gives the raw score means and standard deviations for the subscales of the MDI, indicates groups that were significantly different on the Scheffé analysis.

# Table 1. Post Hoc Comparisons of Means and Standard Deviations of Four Diagnoses on Ten Depressive Symptoms

| Subscale | Conduct Disorder | | Other | | Mixed | | Depressed | |
|---|---|---|---|---|---|---|---|---|
| | Mean | Standard Deviation | Mean | Standard Deviation | Mean | Standard Deviation | Mean | Standard Deviation |
| Sad Mood | 3.27[a] | 2.01 | 4.45[a] | 3.75 | 8.50[b] | 2.07 | 10.50[b] | 2.76 |
| Social Introversion | 3.36[a] | 3.11 | 6.45[a,c] | 3.42 | 8.80[b,c] | 2.62 | 10.30[b] | 2.21 |
| Self-Esteem | 3.72 | 2.79 | 6.82[a] | 2.96 | 8.10[a] | 1.79 | 8.30[a] | 1.57 |
| Irritability | 1.73 | 1.73 | 5.36[a] | 3.98 | 8.60[a,b] | 2.87 | 9.30[b] | 2.36 |
| Cognitive Difficulty | 3.45[a] | 3.39 | 4.36[a] | 3.69 | 8.60[a] | 3.24 | 7.10[a] | 2.92 |
| Energy Level | 0.91 | 0.94 | 5.45[a] | 3.08 | 5.90[a] | 2.51 | 8.00[a] | 2.94 |
| Learned Helplessness | 2.09 | 2.34 | 5.55[a] | 3.44 | 7.20[a] | 1.93 | 8.30[a] | 2.21 |
| Instrumental Helplessness | 1.64 | 1.12 | 4.73 | 3.32 | 8.80[a] | 2.29 | 9.00[a] | 2.00 |
| Guilt | 2.00[a] | 1.26 | 3.36[a] | 3.35 | 8.00[b] | 2.75 | 7.80[b] | 2.29 |
| Pessimism | 3.64[a] | 2.25 | 4.91[a,b] | 3.33 | 7.50[b] | 2.46 | 6.50[a,b] | 1.90 |

*Note*: The higher the score on each subscale, the greater the severity of symptomatology.
[a,b,c]Groups with the same superscripts are not significantly different from each other.

To extend our exploration of the role of depressive symptoms in the description of these four diagnostic groups, a discriminant analysis predicting group membership was performed, with MDI subscales as the independent variables. Discriminant analysis attempts to identify a set of variables that can classify cases (or patients) into distinct categories. Rao's V was selected as the criterion method, because it produces the greatest overall separation for the four groups. Two significant canonical discriminant functions were derived, which used four subscales of the MDI. The first function was significant at $p < .001$ with a $X^2(12) = 64.32$. This function, apparently a severity of depression factor, was characterized by positive weights on all four depression symptoms, with the highest loadings on energy level and instrumental helplessness (Table 2). In Figure 3, the horizontal axis represents this severity of depression function. A higher score indicates increased depression, as measured by all four symptoms. Severity of depression appears to separate the mixed and the depressed groups from the conduct-disordered and the "other" groups. On this horizontal axis, we find a pattern that resembles the relationships depicted in Figures 1 and 2.

A second function was significant at $p < .05$ with a $X^2(6) = 14.68$. The standardized coefficients for this second function (Table 2) indicate that the function is characterized by high loadings for sad mood and energy level and by negative coefficients for instrumental helplessness and guilt. This function, passive depression, is represented in Figure 3 by the vertical axis. A high score indicates increased passive depression. The passive depression failed to separate the mixed group from the group with other diagnoses, but it did separate the depression and the conduct-disordered groups. Hence, Figure 3 provides a graph-theoretic representation of the four diagnostic groups as defined by the two functions.

Table 3 indicates that, for the current sample, these two functions predicted group classifications with an overall accuracy rate of 78.6 percent. The best prediction (100 percent) was for the conduct-disordered group,

### Table 2. Standardized Coefficients for Four Depressive Symptoms on Two Significant Functions Maximizing the Separation of Several Diagnostic Groups

| Scale | Function 1 (Severity of Depression) | Function 2 (Passive Depression) |
|---|---|---|
| Sad Mood | 0.123 | 0.569 |
| Energy Level | 0.457 | 0.794 |
| Instrumental Helplessness | 0.559 | − 0.384 |
| Guilt | 0.289 | − 0.846 |

Note: The four symptoms contributed significantly to the two functions when Rao's V was used as a criterion to maximize discrimination of four diagnostic groups. Low self-esteem, irritability, learned helplessness, pessimism, social introversion, and cognitive difficulty did not contribute significantly to the analysis, so the coefficients for these variables were not computed.

Table 3. Predicted Group Membership for Four Diagnostic
Groups Using Significant Discriminant Functions

| Actual Group | N | Depressed | Conduct-Disordered | Mixed | Other |
|---|---|---|---|---|---|
| | | | *Predicted Group Membership* | | |
| Depressed | 10 | 7 (70%) | 0 (0%) | 1 (10%) | 2 (20%) |
| Conduct-Disordered | 11 | 0 (0%) | 11 (100%) | 0 (0%) | 0 (0%) |
| Mixed | 10 | 2 (20%) | 0 (0%) | 8 (80%) | 0 (0%) |
| Other | 11 | 0 (0%) | 2 (18.2%) | 2 (18.2%) | 7 (63.6%) |

Figure 3. Relationships Among the Four Diagnostic Groups as
Defined by Two Discriminant Functions

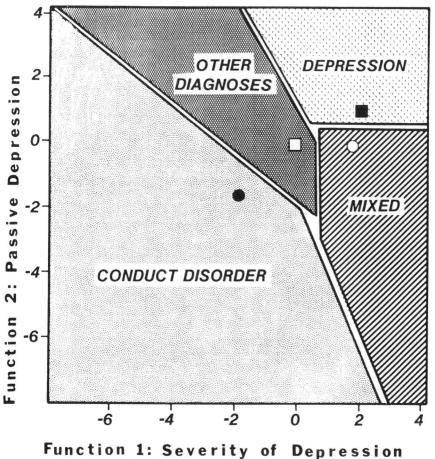

Function 1: Severity of Depression

*Note:* In the discriminant analysis, the severity of depression function, represented by the x axis, and the passive depression function, represented by the y axis, distinguished the four diagnostic groups. The two functions were derived from patterns of scores on sad mood, energy level, guilt, and helplessness.

while diagnostic errors for the mixed group were limited to two cases misclassified as having depression only.

## Discussion

Results from the study reported here most clearly support the third theoretical orientation, represented by DSM-III, Cytryn and others (1980), and Cantwell and Carlson (1983). The first position—that depression is not a useful or feasible diagnosis for youths—is difficult to disprove. However, we demonstrated that patients with DSM-III diagnoses of depression were more symptomatic than other adolescent patients and that the self-reported depressive symptoms provide independent corroboration of the interview-based diagnoses. This does not provide theoretical leverage to demonstrate that the view of depression as a distinct diagnosis has practical advantage. A nomological network of variables (for example, family history, biological markers, responses to treatment) must be explored in relation to depression as a diagnosis and depressive symptomatology. Strober (1983) conducted a study of this nature.

Our data do provide theoretical leverage to evaluate the notion of masked depression. At least in the area of depressive symptoms, patients with a diagnosis of depression, whether or not there is a second diagnosis of conduct disorder, are more severely depressed than patients who are diagnosed only as conduct-disordered. Patients with both diagnoses are very similar to adolescent patients who have only the diagnosis of depression (Figure 1). The graph-theoretic representation of the four diagnostic groups in Figure 3 demonstrates that diagnoses of depression alone and of conduct disorder alone can be differentiated most easily using the MDI symptoms. The mixed group was difficult to differentiate from the group with depression alone. The high classification rate is comparable to or better than that of many current diagnostic studies. However, these results should be viewed with caution until they can be cross-validated.

Lack of energy and sad mood appear to be central symptoms in differentiating adolescents with depression from adolescents with conduct disorders. Patients reporting more instrumental helplessness and relatively less sad mood and lack of energy may be likely to have a conduct disorder. Patients with diagnoses of both depression and conduct disorder were virtually indistinguishable on depressive symptom patterns when compared with adolescent inpatients with the diagnosis of depression alone.

Finally, these findings have practical implications. Adolescents with conduct disorders may or may not also be depressed, and treatment decisions should be tailored to the symptom picture. Many depressed patients also present with behavior problems that are sufficient to merit the additional diagnosis of conduct disorder. For this group of patients, depression is masked by the conduct disorder only if striking behavior problems distract the diagnostician from the affective disorder.

## References

Beck, A. T. *Depression: Clinical, Experimental, and Theoretical Aspects.* New York: Hoeber, 1967.

Berndt, D. J. "How Valid Are the Subscales of the Multiscore Depression Inventory?" *Journal of Clinical Psychology,* 1981, *37,* 564–570.

Berndt, D. J., Kaiser, C. F., and van Aalst, F. "Depression and Self-Actualization in Gifted Adolescents." *Journal of Clinical Psychology,* 1982, *38,* 142–150.

Berndt, D. J., Petzel, T., and Berndt, S. M. "Development and Evaluation of a Multiscore Depression Inventory." *Journal of Personality Assessment,* 1980, *44,* 396–404.

Berndt, D. J., Petzel, T., and Kaiser, C. F. "Evaluation of a Short Form of the Multiscore Depression Inventory." *Journal of Consulting and Clinical Psychology,* 1983, *51,* 790–791.

Berndt, D. J., Schwartz, S., and Kaiser, C. F. "Readability of Self-Report Depression Inventories." *Journal of Consulting and Clinical Psychology,* 1983, *51,* 627–628.

Berndt, D. J., and Berndt, S. M. "Relationship of Mild Depression to Psychological Deficit in College Students." *Journal of Clinical Psychology,* 1980, *36,* 868–873.

Berndt, S. M., Berndt, D. J., and Byars, W. D. "A Multi-Institutional Study of Depression in Family Practice." *Journal of Family Practice,* 1983, *16,* 83–87.

Cantwell, D., and Carlson, G. *Affective Disorders in Childhood and Adolescence.* New York: Spectrum, 1983.

Chambers, W., Puig-Antich, J., and Tabrize, M. A. "The Ongoing Development of the Kiddie-SADS." Paper presented at the annual meeting of the American Academy of Child Psychiatry, San Diego, October 1978.

Cytryn, L., and McKnew, D. "Factors Influencing the Changing Clinical Expression of the Depressive Process in Children." *American Journal of Psychiatry,* 1974, *131,* 879–881.

Cytryn, L., McKnew, D., and Bunney, W. E. "Diagnosis of Depression in Children: A Reassessment." *American Journal of Psychiatry,* 1980, *137,* 22–25.

Evans, J. *Adolescent and Preadolescent Psychiatry.* London: Academic Press, 1982.

Glaser, K. "Masked Depression in Children and Adolescents." *American Journal of Psychotherapy,* 1967, *21,* 565–574.

Joy, D. "Viewing a Rape: The Psychological Costs to Crisis Intervention Volunteers." Paper presented at the 89th annual meeting of the American Psychological Association, Los Angeles, August 1981.

Kovacs, M., and Beck, A. T. "An Empirical-Clinical Approach Towards a Definition of Childhood Depression." In J. Schulterbrandt and A. Raskin (Eds.), *Depression in Childhood: Diagnosis, Treatment, and Conceptual Models.* New York: Raven Press, 1977.

Lesse, S. (Ed.). *Masked Depression.* New York: Aronson, 1974.

Lubin, B. *Depression Adjective Checklists: Manual.* San Diego: Educational and Industrial Testing Service, 1967.

Petzel, T. P., and Berndt, D. J. "Personality Correlates of Depressive Symptoms." Manuscript in preparation, 1983.

Seligman, M. E. P. *Helplessness.* San Francisco: W. H. Freeman, 1975.

Spiegel, R. "Anger and Acting Out as Depressive Equivalents." In S. Lesse (Ed.), *Masked Depression.* New York: Aronson, 1974.

Strober, M. "Clinical and Biological Perspectives on Depressive Disorders in Adolescence." In D. Cantwell and G. Carlson (Eds.), *Affective Disorders in Childhood and Adolescence.* New York: Spectrum, 1983.

Stuckey, M. "The Experience of Depression in Eating-Disordered Women." Unpublished doctoral dissertation, Northwestern University, 1981.

Toolan, J. M. "Depression in Children and Adolescents." *American Journal of Orthopsychiatry,* 1962, *32,* 404–414.

Werry, J. S., Methven, R. J., Fitzpatrick, J., and Dixon, H. "The Interrater Reliability of DSM-III in Children." *Journal of Abnormal child Psychology*, 1983, *11*, 341–354.

Zung, W. W. K. "A Self-Rating Depression Scale." *Archives of General Psychiatry*, 1965, *12*, 63–70.

*David J. Berndt is director of the Adolescent Disorders Laboratory at Michael Reese Hospital and Medical Center and research associate (assistant professor) in the Department of Psychiatry at the University of Chicago Pritzker School of Medicine.*

*David Zinn is director of child and adolescent psychiatry at Michael Reese Hospital and Medical Center and clinical associate professor in the Department of Psychiatry at the University of Chicago Pritzker School of Medicine.*

*Distinct patterns of self-image characterize adolescents*
*with different DSM-III diagnoses.*

# Psychopathology and Adolescent Self-Image

*Linda Koenig*
*Kenneth I. Howard*
*Daniel Offer*
*Michael Cremerius*

This chapter explores the ways in which self-image profiles can distinguish adolescents with different psychiatric disturbances. While it has long been the goal of both researchers and clinicians to discern the differences among psychopathologies, rarely has the patient's own self-view been used in making such distinctions, although the practice appears to have many advantages: It would enable us to learn about an additional aspect of psychiatric disturbances, the disturbances in the patient's self-concept. This information would help clinicians in making differential diagnoses. Moreover, as Offer and others (1981) note, understanding self-image differences would increase our predictive power. That is, knowing how adolescents feel about themselves would indicate how they will behave. Finally, such information would give therapists empathic access to the self as teenagers experience it. Such access could facilitate communication and thereby improve the relationship between therapists and adolescent patients.

The authors thank the Adolescent Research Fund of Michael Reese Hospital and Eric Ostrov for their support.

D. Offer, E. Ostrov, K. I. Howard (Eds.). *Patterns of Adolescent Self-Image.* New Directions
for Mental Health Services, no. 22. San Francisco: Jossey-Bass, June 1984.

A great deal of research has been done on the relationship between psychiatric illness and self-esteem. In general, patients who are diagnosed as neurotic and who experience high anxiety have lower scores on measures of self-esteem than normal subjects do. Wylie (1979) reviews this evidence. However, global self-esteem or self-regard is only one facet of the total picture, and it cannot be considered a sufficient construct for understanding psychiatric illness. Development of the Tennessee Self-Concept Scale (TSCS) (Fitts, 1965) made possible sophisticated analysis of the relationship between self-image and mental health. That instrument, which contains a wide variety of scales, yields fifteen subscores. As a result, self-concept is represented not as a single global score but as a profile depicting various areas of functioning. This important addition to self-concept research allowed investigators to describe and compare patients of different diagnostic groups. In a subsequent publication, Fitts (1972) presents a TSCS profile for every DSM-I diagnostic category. While this work represents an important step toward relating psychopathology to self-concept, it is based on the DSM-I classification system, which is twice removed from the system now in use.

Empirical research on adolescent self-concept has focused primarily on self-esteem. The relationship between high anxiety and low self-esteem observed in adults was found to hold for adolescents as well (Rosenberg, 1965; Long and others, 1970; Ornes, 1970, cited in Thompson, 1972). In addition, low self-esteem has also been related to depression in adolescents (Harrow and others, 1968; Battle, 1980). However, self-esteem alone will not discriminate normal from disturbed teenagers. Lossner (1971, cited in Thompson, 1972) used the TSCS to compare teenagers selected at random both with teenagers who were behaviorally maladjusted and with teenagers who were free of personality and behavioral maladjustment. Lossner found that the three groups showed similar self-esteem scores but that there were distinguishing differences among their profiles.

Theoretical work has pointed to the importance of self during adolescence (Erikson, 1950, 1968). As a result, many researchers have investigated the relationship between identity and adjustment in older adolescents (Bronson, 1959; Block, 1961; Rasmussen, 1964; Marcia, 1966; Hauser and Shapiro, 1973). Engel (1959) found that self-concept is a relatively stable attribute from adolescence onward. Nevertheless, most of the research linking psychiatric illness and self-concept has been done on adults (Rogers and Dymond, 1954; Friedman, 1955; Zucherman and Monashkin, 1957). Until recently, there has been little empirical work investigating specific psychiatric disturbances and self-image in adolescents.

Interest in the self-image of adolescents with specific behavioral disturbances has grown, but it is often difficult to compare the results of these studies, since different measures are used to operationalize self-image. Describing the psychological profile of runaways, Nilson (1981, p. 32) states that all the subjects in her sample had "a very poor self-image" and that they felt "defective, torn apart, ugly, powerless, dumb, criminal, and so forth." These findings were gleaned from extensive psychological batteries as well as from family interviews. Rosengren (1961) employed a social conception of self to evaluate boys diagnosed as passive aggressive personality–aggressive type. These boys displayed behaviors usually described as acting out. Using the Self-Definition Test in this longitudinal study, Rosengren found that boys whose behavior showed the most change from symptomatic to nonsymptomatic also showed the most change in their views of themselves.

Perhaps the syndrome that has received the most attention in relation to self-concept is that of delinquency. Studies by Reckless and others (1956) and Scarpitti (1971) suggest that a positive self-concept can act as a buffer that insulates a boy against delinquency. Scheurer (1971, cited in Thompson, 1972) found that TSCS profiles could distinguish delinquent from nondelinquent boys, and research using the OSIQ has shown that juvenile delinquents, normal subjects, and other emotionally disturbed adolescents have different self-concept profiles (Offer and others, 1979; Offer and Howard, 1972).

As Offer and others (1981) have noted, the OSIQ can be used to differentiate between normal and deviant adolescents and to elucidate the nature of the relationship between self-image and psychopathology. However, it has also been shown that the OSIQ can discriminate between different types of deviance. In a study conducted in Ireland, Brennan and O'Loidein (1980) compared hospitalized adolescents in four groups: psychotic, adjustment reaction, miscellaneous disturbed, and total disturbed less psychotics. Employing the overall mean score, these investigators could differentiate each disturbed group from the normals. Moreover, the psychotic group could be distinguished from the adjustment reaction group, and the adjustment reaction group could be distinguished from the rest of the disturbed group. The overall mean score showed no difference between the adjustment reaction group and the miscellaneous disturbed group or between the miscellaneous disturbed group and the combined psychotic and adjustment reaction group.

In light of the research cited earlier, we felt that the OSIQ was an appropriate instrument to use in a study comparing the self-images of teenagers with different psychiatric diagnoses. The OSIQ was designed specifically for use with adolescents, and it evaluates specific areas of functioning as well as global functioning. In addition, there is a standardized normal reference sample with which the disturbed samples can be compared. Thus, specific deficits in self-image can be identified in relation to the functioning of normals.

Moreover, research evaluating the clinical utility of the OSIQ in psychiatric settings has compared it with the more traditional measures of psychopathology. Two studies have compared the OSIQ with the Minnesota Multiphasic Personality Inventory (MMPI). Coché and Taylor (1974) correlated the scales of the two instruments and found that 27 percent of their correlations were significant at the .05 level. Dudley and others (1981) extended the investigation by computing the correlations within and between instruments as well as by factor analyzing their data to summarize the sources of variance common to both. The same authors also report the relationships between various background variables and test scores. It appears that the OSIQ taps important indexes of psychopathology. The results reported in this chapter will add to this growing body of information on the applicability of the OSIQ to evaluations of psychiatric disturbance among adolescents.

## Methods and Procedures

*Subjects.* The subjects in our study were adolescents between the ages of twelve and nineteen from six psychiatric facilities in the United States. Four of these facilities were hospitals located in the Chicago metropolitan area; two were private with short-term treatment programs (generally less than three months), one was private with long-term treatment, and one was a state psychiatric facility with long-term treatment. The fifth facility was a university hospital located in Wisconsin, while the sixth was a private hospital with long-term treatment located in Texas. Our sample also contained a group of adolescents from California who had been defined as depressed as a result of their scores on the Beck Depression Inventory (Beck and others, 1961). Our samples were collected between 1970 and 1983 by independent investigators.

*Measures.* With OSIQ scores, investigators supplied us with the patient's psychiatric diagnosis as reported in the patient's medical record. On the basis of these diagnoses, subjects were placed in one of four DSM-III diagnostic categories: depression (bipolar disorder, depressed, 296.5; major depression, single, 296.2, or recurrent, 296.3; dysthymic disorder, 300.40; or atypical depression, 296.82), conduct disorder (312.00, 312.10, 312.23, 312.21, or 312.90), eating disorder (307.10 or 307.51), and psychosis (schizophrenia, 295.1, 295.2, 295.3, 295.9, or 295.6; schizophreniform disorder, 295.40; schizoaffective disorder, 295.70; pervasive developmental disorder — childhood onset, 299.9; or major depression with psychotic features, 296.24 or 296.34). One sample contained DSM-II diagnoses. These patients were used only if their diagnosis could unambiguously be converted into a DSM-III diagnosis in accordance with the comparison table in DSM-III.

Many subjects had multiple diagnoses. To cope with this problem, subjects were included under each applicable diagnosis tested. To evaluate whether this categorizing procedure distorted results, comparisons were also made between patients with only one diagnosis. These comparisons did not differ appreciably from those using the patients with multiple diagnoses, so the original groupings were retained.

## Analyses and Results

Each subject's questionnaire was standard scored, and the means for every scale within each of the four diagnostic categories were computed. Based on these means, a standard score profile was generated for each diagnostic group. A five-point (rounded score) difference was set as the criterion for judging a score to be different from the normal mean. This criterion was selected for two reasons. First, using the *t* statistic, this cutoff represented no less than the .05 level of significance. (A ten-point criterion was set for the psychosis group in order to achieve a statistically significant difference at the .05 level.) Second, we felt that at least this magnitude of difference was necessary for the deviation to be psychologically meaningful.

*Depression.* Figure 1 shows that the depressed adolescents displayed self-image deficits in five areas of functioning. In the area of the psychological self, the depressed adolescents scored low in the Impulse Control scale (45) and the Emotional Tone scale (44). The Morals scale (44), an aspect of the social self, was notably low, while the Family Relationships scale (40), an aspect of the familial self, was markedly low. In the area of the coping self, the depressed adolescents scored low on the Mastery of the External World scale (45). On six scales—Body and Self-Image (49), Social Relationships (48), Vocational and Educational Goals (49), Sexual Attitudes (51), Psychopathology (46), and Superior Adjustment (48)—the depressed adolescents did not deviate significantly from the normal subjects.

The depression profile appears to be characterized by the very low family relationships score. These adolescents reported a conflictual atmos-

**Figure 1. Offer Self-Image Questionnaire Standard Score Profile for Adolescents with the Diagnosis of Depression (*N* = 213)**

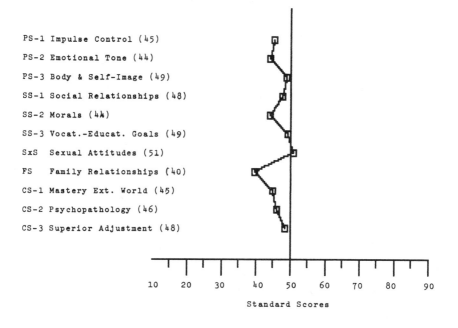

*Note:* Numbers in parentheses are standard score values for each scale. PS = Psychological Self, SS = Social Self, SxS = Sexual Self, FS = Familial Self, CS = Coping Self. Data collected by Berndt, Cremerius, Gibbs, Koenig, Looney, Marohn, Saper, and Zinn.

phere in the home and indicated that they did not get along well with their parents. For them, this, not depressed affect, represented the greatest of their problems. However, depressed mood still remained a problem for them. They lacked affective stability, and they experienced distress over their inability to control their low affect and anxious feelings. In addition, they reported poor impulse control. Their tolerance of frustration was low, and they lacked the ability to ward off pressures that they were experiencing from their internal and external environments. While they were comfortable with the bodily changes that occur during adolescence and while they reported normal attitudes towards sexuality, their psychological functioning seemed to be characterized by a lack of control over their feelings and behaviors. This problem was exacerbated by their perceived estrangement from their families and by their inability to use the family system as a source of support.

Contrary to theories of depression that stress the role of guilt resulting from a harsh superego, these adolescents did not report feelings of guilt or remorse. In fact, their social functioning was impaired by their poorly developed superegos. They felt a less than normal sense of responsibility to or concern for others, and they endorsed such items as "Telling the truth means nothing to me" and "I do not care how my actions affect others as long as I gain something." Nevertheless, they reported that they had good peer relationships, which were satisfying to them. In addition, they seemed to function well within the school system and to be planning appropriately for their vocational futures.

In regard to the coping abilities of these teenagers, it appears that they were unable to master their immediate environment. Typical of depressive symptomatology, they could not visualize themselves as completing the tasks with which they were faced, and they endorsed such items as "I have no talent whatsoever" and "I find life an endless series of problems without solution in sight." Their strength lies in the facts that they had generally good ego strength and that they did not experience overt psychotic symptoms.

It is not surprising that these adolescents experienced depressed affect and hopelessness over task completion. It is possible that their depressed feelings were the result of their having poor impulse control. Similarly, hopelessness related to task completion might also be the result of their having poor impulse control: If they lack the ability to forsake short-term pleasures in favor of long-term goals, they cannot complete important tasks. It is possible to view the poor family atmosphere that these adolescents reported as either a cause or a result of their depression. They may be responding to a conflictual family atmosphere, or the conflict within the family system may be the result of the strain caused by their depression.

It should be noted that some of these findings may be modified when age and sex are taken into consideration. Preliminary findings of age-by-sex interactions point to a tendency for younger depressed males to score consistently lower than older depressed males. It is possible that younger males need to show more disturbance before they are hospitalized. However, it is also possible that depression simply becomes more ego-syntonic as the male adolescent grows older. In either case, age and gender may be important variables in understanding the self-image disturbances of adolescents with depression.

*Conduct Disorder.* Figure 2 shows the OSIQ profile for the adolescents with conduct disorders. In the area of the familial self, these adolescents displayed functioning that was significantly lower than that of normal subjects. Their score on the Family Relationships scale (28) represents the lowest score in this area for all groups studied. In the area of the psychological self, the conduct-disordered adolescents displayed deficits on the Impulse Control scale (45) and on the Emotional Tone scale (43). In the area of the social self, they showed a marked deficit on the Morals scale (42) as well as a deficit on the Vocational and Educational Goals scale (45). In addition, one aspect of their coping self was disturbed, as their low Superior Adjustment scale score (44) indicates. Their scores on five scales — Body and Self-Image (50), Social Relationships (47), Sexual Attitudes (52), Mastery of the External World (46), and Psychopathology (46) — did not deviate significantly from those of normals.

Conduct-disordered adolescents were characterized by severely disturbed family interactions. Apparently, their behavioral maladjustment and

**Figure 2. Offer Self-Image Questionnaire Standard Score Profile for Adolescents with the Diagnosis of Conduct Disorder (N = 68)**

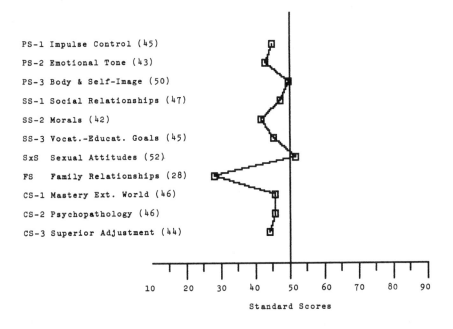

*Note:* Numbers in parentheses are standard score values for each scale. PS = Psychological Self, SS = Social Self, SxS = Sexual Self, FS = Familial Self, CS = Coping Self. Data collected by Berndt, Cremerius, Koenig, Marohn, Saper, and Zinn.

their defiance of parental authority caused a great deal of tension in the home. They negatively endorsed such items as "I can count on my parents most of the time" and "I think I will be a source of pride to my parents in the future," and their reports indicated a serious breakdown in communication between parent and child.

These teenagers also had difficulty in two areas of psychological functioning, impulse control and emotional tone. Like depressives, they experienced feelings of depression and anxiety, and they experienced distress over their inability to control their emotional tone. In addition, unable to ward off or delay the pressures that they experienced, they often acted on impulse. They had low tolerance of frustration, and they needed help both in developing cognitive and behavioral control and in learning how to delay gratification for higher-level goals. Like their depressed counterparts, they were not uncomfortable or overly concerned with the bodily changes that they were experiencing, and their sexual attitudes were similar to those expressed by normal teenagers. However, they seemed to be distressed by their general lack of control over their moods and behaviors.

Again like depressives, these adolescents showed poorly developed superego functioning, which is not surprising, since they manifested their disturbances by acting out against social norms and rules. Again, they felt little duty or obligation to others. Moreover, they did not function well within the school system, and they endorsed such items as "Only stupid people work" and "School and studying mean very little to me." They were not fulfilling the adolescent task of learning and planning for a vocational future, indicating that the adolescent with a conduct disorder probably needs special help reintegrating into the school environment as well as guidance in vocational planning. Although these teenagers showed deficits in both areas of social functioning, it should be noted that they reported experiencing adequate peer relationships.

The adolescents with conduct disorders differed from normal subjects in one area of coping skills, superior adjustment, which is a measure of ego strength. Although they continued to perform, they experienced an internal lack of confidence. This contrasts with the depressed adolescents, who experienced hopelessness and did not act at all. They endorsed such items as "I am certain I will not be able to assume responsibilities for myself in the future" and "If I were separated from all the people I know, I feel that I would not be able to make a go of it." However, they continued to respond to their immediate environment, and they did not show a significant level of psychotic symptomatology.

*Eating Disorder.* Figure 3 shows the OSIQ profile for the adolescents with eating disorders. As Casper and others (1981) and Swift (1981) found, the girls with eating disorders showed a number of serious disturbances. The profile indicates that there were disturbances in all areas of the psychological self, ranging from mild disturbance on the Impulse Control scale (44) and moderate disturbance on the Body and Self-Image scale (35) to severe disturbance on the Emotional Tone scale (30). These teenagers also displayed a large deviation from normal on the Social Relationships scale (33), which is part of the social self. In the area of the coping self, they showed a marked disturbance on the scales measuring Mastery of the External World (41) and Psychopathology (39). Finally, the deviation of the greatest magnitude lies in the area of the sexual self, as indicated by their score on the Sexual Attitudes scale (29).

Unlike the other disturbed groups that we studied, the adolescents with eating disorders resembled the normals with respect to the Family Relationships scale (50). In addition, they did not deviate significantly on the Vocational and Educational Goals scale (54), the Morals scale (53), or the Superior Adjustment scale (50).

The adolescents with eating disorders displayed by far the most deviant profile both in terms of the number of deviant scales and of the magnitude of deviation on these scales. These adolescents were characterized by extremely depressed scores on the Body and Self-Image scale and the Sexual Attitudes scale — scales on which no other deviant groups showed disturbance. They reported experiencing an awkwardness about their body and the physical

**Figure 3. Offer Self-Image Questionnaire Standard Score Profile for Adolescents with the Diagnosis of Eating Disorder (N = 71)**

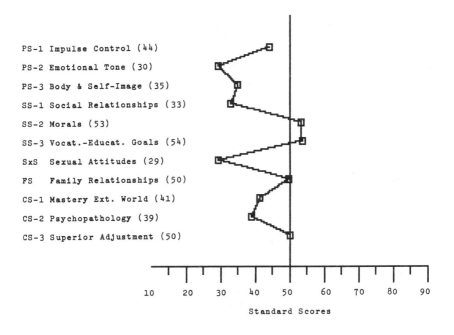

*Note:* Numbers in parentheses are standard score values for each scale. PS = Psychological Self, SS = Social Self, SxS = Sexual Self, FS = Familial Self, CS = Coping Self. Data collected by Berndt, Casper, Koenig, Saper, Swift, and Zinn.

changes that were occurring, and they endorsed such items as "I frequently feel ugly and unattractive" and "Very often I think I am not at all the person I would like to be." This is not unexpected, considering the physical nature of their disturbance. In addition, low scores on the Body and Self-Image scale can also represent confusion about body boundaries, and the low score that our study found supports research suggesting that adolescents with eating disorders suffer from body boundary disturbances (Strober and Goldenberg, 1981). The low scores of these adolescents on the Sexual Attitudes scale supports theories that view eating disorders as a flight from emerging sexuality. These girls reported an extremely conservative attitude toward sex. They endorsed such items as "It is very hard for a teenager to know how to handle sex in the right way" and "Thinking or talking about sex frightens me."

These teenagers were disturbed in all areas of the psychological self. In addition to their concerns over bodily changes, they reported feeling depressed and anxious, and they were distressed by their lack of control over their mood states. They also indicated that they had low tolerance of frustration and that they often acted impulsively.

Two areas of coping ability were also disturbed. Although these adolescents expressed confidence in their ability to cope with the world, they had problems in dealing with their immediate environment. They were unable to foresee themselves as being successful at completing tasks. They also reported experiencing psychotic symptoms and endorsed such items as "I feel empty emotionally most of the time." and "When I enter a new room, I have a strange and funny feeling." These reports support clinical observations that anorexics display psychotic symptoms during periods of malnutrition, symptoms that remit when proper nutrition is restored (Casper, 1983).

In two areas of social functioning, the adolescents with eating disorders appeared to be normal: No difficulties were reported in the area of superego development or of educational and vocational planning. These teenagers felt a sense of duty and responsibility to others, and they functioned well within their school environment. However, they scored quite low in the area of social relationships, endorsing such items as "I usually feel out of place at picnics and parties" and "I find it extremely hard to make friends." This scale is a measure of friendship patterns, and the very low score indicates that these teenagers felt lonely and isolated and that they were estranged from their peers.

Interestingly, girls with eating disorders did not differ from normal girls on the Family Relationships scale. This differentiates them from the other disturbed groups that we studied. These teenagers did not express their pathology in that area, and in spite of what was occurring psychologically, they did not report outright conflict within the family. They reported that they held positive feelings toward their families. Based on theoretical perspectives, we can speculate that these girls did not successfully complete the process of separation and individuation (Masterson, 1977) and that they are in fact enmeshed with their families. (Being too close to their families might also account for their difficulty in dealing with peers of their own age.) While there may indeed be a problem within the family system, clinicians might be wise to note that such patients do not see their problems as such and to take this into consideration when planning a treatment approach.

As in the case of adolescents with depression and conduct disorders, age may be an important variable in the self-image disturbances of girls with eating disorders. In our sample, older girls tended to score lower than younger girls (Casper and others, 1981). It is possible that these disturbances increase as the adolescent approaches young adulthood and the tasks of separating from their family and assuming adult responsibilities.

*Psychosis.* Figure 4 displays the OSIQ profile of the psychotic teenagers. Although we must exercise caution when interpreting a profile based on fourteen subjects, it can be seen that several scales deviated by ten points or more. The psychotic adolescents scored low on the Emotional Tone scale (39), the Social Relationships scale (36), the Family Relationships scale (37) and the Psychopathology scale (40). On seven scales—Impulse Control (47), Body and Self-Image (48), Morals (41), Vocational and Educational Goals (46), Sexual Attitudes (50), Mastery of the External World (47), and Superior Adjustment (46)—their scores did not differ significantly from those of normals.

**Figure 4. Offer Self-Image Questionnaire Standard Score Profile for Adolescents with the Diagnosis of Psychosis (*N* = 14)**

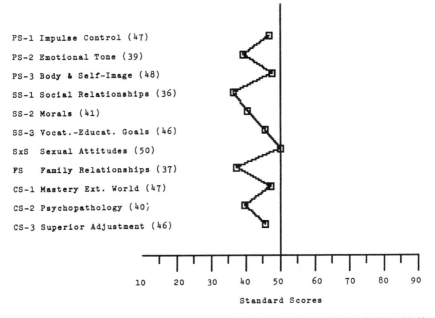

*Note:* Numbers in parentheses are standard score values for each scale. PS = Psychological Self, SS = Social Self, SxS = Sexual Self, FS = Familial Self, CS = Coping Self. Data collected by Berndt, Koenig, Marohn, Saper, and Zinn.

The subjects in our sample of psychotic teenagers reported experiencing difficulties in four areas of functioning. In the area of the psychological self, these adolescents reported feeling depressed and anxious, and they were distressed by their lack of affective control. However, they reported no difficulties tolerating frustration or delaying gratification, and in contrast to research reporting body boundary disturbance in psychotics (Quinlan and Harrow, 1974), they reported no awkwardness over their body or confusion about body boundaries.

Social relationships were also a problem for these teenagers. They reported poor peer relationships, and as a result they felt lonely and isolated from others. It would seem that their severe pathology stood in the way of their ability to form friendships and interact socially. However, they were not deviant in terms of superego functioning, and they appeared to be functioning adequately within the school environment.

Attitudes toward sex within this group did not differ from those of normals, but like most of the other disturbed adolescents in our sample, these teenagers reported conflictual relationships between themselves and their parents. In the area of coping abilities, they did not have difficulty in coping with their immediate environment, nor did they lack the internal confidence needed to deal with the world. However, they did report experiencing the severe psychotic symptoms characteristic of the group that they represented.

## Conclusion

As the profiles included in this chapter make clear, not only did the emotionally disturbed adolescents in our sample show self-image deficits, but each diagnostic group displayed its own particular pattern of disturbance. It is also apparent that the four groups represented in our sample shared some common features. For example, all the profiles show a lowering in the Emotional Tone scale. This scale, which contains such items as "I enjoy life" and "I am so very anxious," measures the degree of affective harmony within the psychic structure. Disturbed adolescents tended to report that they experienced feelings of depression and anxiety and that they were distressed by their lack of control over their moods. In general, the depressed adolescents and the adolescents with conduct disorders were moderately distressed, while the psychotic adolescents and the adolescents with eating disorders were more seriously distressed. While the Emotional Tone scale relates expressly to mood, it appears to tap more than simple depression or anxiety, rather, it appears to be a fairly generalized measure of symptomatology.

Three of our groups — the depressed, the conduct-disordered, and the eating-disordered adolescents — reported that they could not tolerate frustration and that they responded to frustration by acting impulsively. They endorsed such items as "I 'lose my head' easily" and "I get violent if I don't get my way." Apparently, this is not just a problem for teenagers with conduct disorders. All these teenagers acted on impulse, and they all needed help to learn how to generate response alternatives and think in terms of future consequences and long-term goals.

Family relationships were also seriously disturbed for most of the teenagers in our sample. The Family Relationship scale measures the quality of the parent-child relationship as well as the emotional atmosphere in the home. The low scores here indicate that there were serious communication problems within the families of our subjects. The constant conflict and altercations within the family environment were a great source of distress to the adolescents whom we studied, especially to those with conduct disorders. Adolescents with eating disorders were an exception. We suspect that their normal scores on this scale are the result of their being too close to their families. It is possible that they have not successfully separated from their parents and thus that they report positive family relationships, in spite of conflicts over eating, power, authority, and so forth. Since the family is of great importance in the psychological and emotional development of children, it behooves clinicians to take adolescents' reports seriously and to make use of such treatment as family therapy to facilitate communication between children and parents.

Similarities are also evident between pairs of profiles. As already mentioned, the profiles for the depressed and the conduct-disordered adolescents display several similar features, such as disturbances in emotional tone, impulse control, morals, and family relationships. Although both groups differed from normal subjects in coping abilities, the primary distinction seems to lie in the very large family relationships deficit seen in the profile for conduct-disordered subjects. This deficit could be the result of a long history of rule breaking behavior on the part of these adolescents. The child's behavior would strain the family system and thus disrupt the normal home environment. However, it is also possible that the family situation is the determinant of the acting-out behavior. In other words, the way in which the disturbance is manifested would depend on the family environment. Disturbed teenagers who found themselves in a more conflictual interpersonal milieu would respond by acting out, while disturbed teenagers who found themselves in less conflictual situations would respond with depressive symptomatology.

Similarities also exist between psychotic adolescents and adolescents with eating disorders. Both groups scored low on the Social Relationships scale, which indicates that they are having difficulty in maintaining satisfying peer relationships. In addition, both groups scored low on the Psychopathology Scale. Thus, it appears that adolescents with eating disorders may also be experiencing psychotic symptoms.

In conclusion, preliminary investigation seems to indicate that different pathologies are indeed related to different patterns of self-image in adolescents. Future research will need to increase sample sizes and improve the reliability of the diagnostic procedure. Moreover, other means of grouping subjects, such as behavioral obserations or symptom reports, need to be used in addition to structured diagnostic procedures. In this way, the clinical utility of the OSIQ could be enhanced. Nevertheless, the results of our study seem to indicate that self-image is a valuable perspective that can increase our understanding of adolescent psychopathology.

## References

Battle, J. "Relationship Between Self-Esteem and Depression Among High School Students." *Perceptual and Motor Skills,* 1980, *51,* 157–158.

Beck, A. T., Ward, C. H., Mendelson, M., Mock, H., and Erbaugh, J. "An Inventory for Measuring Depression." *Archives of General Psychiatry,* 1961, *4,* 561–571.

Block, J. "Ego Identity, Role Variability, and Adjustment." *Journal of Consulting Psychology,* 1961, *25* (5), 392–397.

Brennan, T. G., and O'Loideain, D. S. "A Comparison of Normal and Disturbed Adolescent Offer Self-Image Questionnaire Responses in an Irish Cultural Setting." *Journal of Youth and Adolescence,* 1980, *9* (1), 11–18.

Bronson, G. "Identity Diffusion in Late Adolescents." *Journal of Abnormal and Social Psychology,* 1959, *9,* 414–417.

Casper, R. C., Offer, D., and Ostrov, E. "The Self-Image of Adolescents with Acute Anorexia Nervosa." *Journal of Pediatrics,* 1981, *98,* 651–656.

Casper, R. C. Personal Communication, 1983.

Coché, E., and Taylor, S. "Correlations Between the Offer Self-Image Questionnaire for Adolescents and the Minnesota Multiphasic Personality Inventory in a Psychiatric Hospital Population." *Journal of Youth and Adolescence,* 1974, *3* (2), 145–152.

Dudley, H. H., Jr., Craig, E. M., and Mason, J. M. "The Measurement of Adolescent Personality: The MMPI and the Offer Self-Image Questionnaire for Adolescents." *Adolescence,* 1981, *16* (62), 453–469.

Engel, M. "The Stability of the Self-Concept in Adolescence." *Journal of Abnormal and Social Psychology,* 1959, *58,* 211–215.

Erikson, E. *Childhood and Society.* New York: Norton, 1950.

Erikson, E. *Identity, Youth, and Crisis.* New York: Norton, 1968.

Fitts, W. H. *Manual for the Tennessee Self-Concept Scale.* Nashville: Counselor Recordings and Tests, 1965.

Fitts, W. H. *The Self-Concept and Psychopathology.* Dede Wallace Center Monograph No. 4. Nashville: Dede Wallace Center, 1972.

Friedman, I. "Phenomenal, Ideal, and Projected Conceptions of the Self." *Journal of Abnormal and Social Psychology,* 1955, *51,* 611–615.

Harrow, M., Fox, D. A., Markhus, K. L., Stillman, R., and Hallowell, C. B. "Changes in Adolescents' Self-Concepts and Their Parents' Perceptions During Psychiatric Hospitalization." *Journal of Nervous and Mental Disease,* 1968, *147* (3), 252–259.

Hauser, S. T., and Shapiro, R. L. "Differentiation of Adolescent Self-Images." *Archives of General Psychiatry,* 1973, *26,* 63–68.

Long, B. H., Ziller, R. C., and Banks, J. "Self-Other Orientations in Institutionalized Behavior-Problem Adolescents." *Journal of Consulting and Clinical Psychology,* 1970, *34* (1), 43–47.

Lossner, A. B., "The Relationship of Self-Concept to Maladjustment in High School Students." Unpublished master's thesis, Murray State University, 1971.

Marcia, J. E. "Development and Validation of Ego Identity Status." *Journal of Personality and Social Psychology,* 1966, *3* (5), 551–558.

Masterson, J. "Primary Anorexia Nervosa in the Borderline Adolescent: An Object Relations View." In P. Hartocolli (Ed.), *Borderline Personality Disorders.* New York: International University Press, 1977.

Nilson, P. "Psychological Profiles of Runaway Children and Adolescents." In C. F. Well and I. R. Stuart (Eds.), *Self-Destructive Behavior in Children and Adolescents.* New York: Van Nostrand Reinhold, 1981.

Offer, D., and Howard, K. I. "An Empirical Analysis of the Offer Self-Image Questionnaire for Adolescents." *Archives of General Psychiatry*, 1972, *27*, 529–537.

Offer, D., Marohn, R. C., and Ostrov, E. *The Psychological World of the Juvenile Delinquent.* New York: Basic Books, 1979.

Offer, D., Ostrov, E., and Howard, K. I. *The Adolescent: A Psychological Self-Portrait.* New York: Basic Books, 1981.

Ornes, E. J. "The Relationship Between Trait Anxiety and Self-Concept." Unpublished master's thesis, Middle Tennessee University, 1970.

Quinlan, D. M., and Harrow, M. "Boundary Disturbances in Schizophrenia." *Journal of Abnormal Psychology*, 1974, *83*, 533–541.

Rasmussen, J. E. "Relationship of Ego Identity of Psychosocial Effectiveness." *Psychological Reports*, 1964, *15*, 815–825.

Reckless, W. C., Dinitz, S., and Murray, E. "Self-Concept as an Insulator Against Delinquency." *American Sociological Review*, 1956, *31*, 744–746.

Rogers, C. R., and Dymond, R. R. *Psychotherapy and Personality Change.* Chicago: University of Chicago Press, 1954.

Rosenberg, M. *Society and the Adolescent Self-Image.* Princeton, N.J.: Princeton University Press, 1965.

Rosengren, W. R. "The Self in the Emotionally Disturbed." *American Journal of Sociology*, 1961, *66*, 454–462.

Scarpitti, F. R. "Delinquent and Nondelinquent Perceptions of Self, Values, and Opportunity." In M. Powell and A. H. Frericks (Eds.), *Reading in Adolescent Psychology.* Minneapolis: Burgess, 1971.

Scheurer, W. E. "Self-Concept: A Comparison of Delinquent and Nondelinquent Adolescents." Unpublished master's thesis, Ball State University, 1971.

Strober, M., and Goldenberg, I. "Ego Boundary Disturbance in Juvenile Anorexia Nervosa." *Journal of Clinical Psychology*, 1981, *37* (2), 433–438.

Swift, W. Personal communication, 1981.

Thompson, W. *Correlates of Self-Concept.* Dede Wallace Center Monograph No. 6. Nashville: Dede Wallace Center, 1972.

Wylie, R. C. *The Self-Concept: Theories and Research on Selected Topics.* Vol. 2. (Rev. ed.) Lincoln: University of Nebraska Press, 1979.

Zucherman, M., and Monashkin, I. "Self-Acceptance and Psychopathology." *Journal of Consulting Psychology, 1957, 21,* 145–148.

*Linda Koenig is a doctoral student in the Department of Psychology at Northwestern University.*

*Kenneth I. Howard is professor of psychology at Northwestern University; professor of psychology at Northwestern University Medical School; senior research consultant in the Department of Psychiatry at Michael Reese Hospital and Medical Center; and senior research consultant at the Institute for Juvenile Research.*

*Daniel Offer is chairman of the Department of Psychiatry at Michael Reese Hospital and Medical Center and professor of psychiatry at the University of Chicago Pritzker School of Medicine.*

*Michael Cremerius is a doctoral student in the Department of Psychology at Loyola University.*

*About 50 percent of disturbed adolescents are not recognized*
*by adults as needing psychiatric help.*

# The Quietly Disturbed Adolescent

*Eric Ostrov*
*Daniel Offer*
*Shirley Hartlage*

This chapter presents preliminary findings about a group of adolescents who have received relatively little attention in the research literature, the quietly disturbed adolescents. By definition, this group consists of teenagers who are emotionally disturbed but who have not yet manifested this disturbance in a way that brings them to the attention of mental health professionals, educators, law enforcement personnel, or even parents. As Chapter One pointed out, past research on adolescents has focused on clinical cases: adolescents seeking or referred for help. More recent empirical work has focused on the vast majority of adolescents who cope well with the changes and tasks attendant on making the change from child to adult (Rosenberg, 1965; Offer and others, 1981; Csikszentmihalyi and Larson, 1984). We know very little about the characteristics of quietly disturbed youth and even less about their numbers. Members of this group often become known only when they emerge from their quietness and loneliness with a sudden desparate act such as suicide or homicide. More likely, these adolescents do not emerge at all. Instead, they live with their problems, and many may carry them into adulthood. Implications can be drawn for treatment only when research clarifies the number of youths in need and the psychiatric problems that they present.

The authors are grateful to the William T. Grant Foundation for its support under grant 82-0855-00.

D. Offer, E. Ostrov, K. I. Howard (Eds.). *Patterns of Adolescent Self-Image.* New Directions for Mental Health Services, no. 22. San Francisco: Jossey-Bass, June 1984.

How prevalent is the quietly disturbed adolescent? The empirical literature indicates that between 10 and 30 percent of all adolescents evince a significant amount of psychiatric disturbance. This chapter will show that there is almost no literature on the specific kinds of psychiatric illness found among disturbed youths in the community. Similarly, there is almost no literature on the prevalence or characteristics of quietly disturbed adolescents. This chapter will present and discuss data that have a bearing on this issue.

An early study conducted by Krupinski and others (1967) in the small Australian town of Heyfield found that 16 percent of the male adolescents and 19 percent of the female adolescents had psychiatrically diagnosable conditions. Adults in Heyfield were also studied, and the researchers found that 23 percent of the male adults and 19 percent of the female adults in that community had psychiatrically diagnosable conditions. A study conducted by Bjornsson (1974) in a Scandinavian industrial town reported a 21 percent prevalence rate of moderate to severe disorder for boys thirteen to fourteen years old and a 14 percent rate for girls of the same ages.

A key series of studies was conducted by Rutter and his colleagues (Graham and Rutter, 1973; Rutter and others, 1976) on the Isle of Wight off the coast of England. The people there lived primarily in small towns and villages. Information was based on individual interviews by psychiatrists and interviews with parents and teachers. According to the authors, "More than a fifth of the boys and girls reported that they felt miserable or depressed, and the same proportion reported great difficulty in sleeping and waking unnecessarily early in the morning" (Rutter and others, 1976, p. 42). Using information from interviews with parents, these authors found that the prevalence of psychiatric disorder among the fourteen-year-olds studied was 13 percent for males and 13 percent for females. Using interviews with the adolescents themselves, the same authors concluded that 16 percent were diagnosable as having psychiatric disorders. Using data from multiple sources, Graham and Rutter (1973, p. 122) concluded that "the corrected prevalence rate for psychiatric disorder in fourteen- to fifteen-year-old children is 21.0 percent." Using information from the mothers of these teenagers about themselves and their husbands, these authors found that the comparable prevalence rate for male and female adults in the families of these adolescents was 8 percent and 12 percent, respectively.

There have been relatively few studies in the United States of the prevalence of emotional disturbance or of the kinds of disturbance among adolescents. This fact has been emphasized by Locksley and Douvan (1979, p. 73): "Although national surveys of the incidence of psychopathology among adolescents have not been conducted as yet, this may be a direction for research ultimately as profitable as those directions heretofore pursued."

Langner and others (1974) conducted a study of the epidemiology of psychiatric illness among adolescents in this country. These authors administered a questionnaire to mothers, who were asked to report on their children's behavior. The sample consisted of 1,034 children between the ages of six and eighteen who were selected at random from a cross section of Manhattan in New York City. Questionnaire results were rated by a psychiatrist for degree of impairment. Results showed extreme impairment for between 17 and 20 percent of the black and Hispanic children and for between 8 and 9 percent of the white children. Unfortunately, the results for adolescents were not reported separately. In the study by Locksley and Douvan (1979), sophomores, juniors, and seniors attending a midwestern urban lower-middle-class high school were asked to complete a self-report questionnaire. To obtain longitudinal data, the questionnaire was readministered to a subsample of the sophomores during their senior year. According to Locksley and Douvan, males reported a significantly higher frequency of aggression and of feelings of resentment than females did, while females reported a significantly higher frequency of feelings of tension and psychosomatic symptoms than males did. The sexes did not differ in their reports of feelings of depression. Unfortunately, Locksley and Douvan did not estimate the prevalence of psychiatric disorder among the adolescents whom they studied.

Other studies conducted in the United States have focused on the incidence of depressive symptoms among adolescents, not on the incidence of psychiatric illness in general. Schoenbach and others (1980) administered a self-report depressive symptom checklist to 384 junior high school students. Responses showed elevated symptom scores among blacks and among whites of low socioeconomic status. The authors did not report prevalence rates of depression, but they did note that adolescents showed similar symptom "persistence;" that is, adolescents and adults reported that they felt symptoms of depression most or all the time during the preceding week at the same rate. The authors note (p. 440) that the results "cast doubt about the adequacy of the developmental explanation for adolescent depressive symptoms, especially persistent ones." Using the Beck Depression Inventory to study small samples of seventh- and eighth-graders from a parochial school in suburban Philadelphia, Albert and Beck (1975) concluded that 31.1 percent of their early-adolescent sample fell into the moderate depressive symptomatology range, and only 2.2 percent fell into the severe range.

Kandel and Davies (1982) also studied the epidemiology of depression among adolescents. Among adolescents between fourteen and eighteen years of age who were representative of public high school students in New York state in 1971–1972, these authors found that adolescents from families with very low incomes were more depressed than adolescents from any other group. Girls were more depressed than boys. The authors also found that levels of self-reported depressive mood were higher among adolescents than among their parents. This generational difference was greater for the females than it was for the males. The authors cite one prevalence rate: Twenty percent of the adolescents reported being much bothered about feeling sad or depressed within the past year.

A review of the literature revealed only one study relevant to the issue of the proportion of psychiatrically ill youths who seek or obtain help. That study, conducted in Britain by Leslie (1974, p. 118) concluded that "the parents of twenty-four out of the sixty-seven children with psychiatric disorder had not sought advice at any time; some did not perceive abnormality, but others did not know of anyone who would help with such problems." Given the findings of Gurin and others (1960) and Veroff and others (1981)—that most adults do not seek professional help even when facing an emotional crisis—it seems likely that many emotionally disturbed youths are not identified as such and that they do not receive help.

To summarize, published studies indicate that a sizable proportion of adolescents manifest psychiatric illness—specifically, clinically significant symptoms of depression. Very few such studies have been conducted in this country. In all countries, the proportion of disturbed adolescents who do not seek or receive help is largely unknown. The study described in this chapter sought to further knowledge in this field.

## Method

*Subjects.* The roster of all students in a Chicago suburban high school was used to select a random sample of one fourteenth of the student body. Since there were 4,530 students at the school, a list of 324 students was obtained. The smallest cell—of male freshmen and sophomores, male juniors and seniors, female freshmen and sophomores, and female juniors and seniors—contained sixty-five students. Sixty-five students were then drawn at random from each of the other cells, yielding a total of 260 students. Questionnaires were mailed to these teenagers together with a request that they fill them out and return them to the investigators. As an incentive to cooperate, the teenagers were promised a $5 gift certificate on return of the completed form that they could use to purchase a record at a local record store. Students who did not respond were called by the investigators to encourage participation. To increase the number of returns, a research assistant went to the homes of the teenagers to encourage them to complete the questionnaires. As a result of these efforts 87 percent of the students sampled provided data.

To make our data base demographically more diverse, we also collected questionnaires from two Roman Catholic high schools located in Chicago. One of these schools, located in a lower-class to lower-middle-class neighborhood, is all male and all black. The other, located in a lower-middle-class to upper-middle-class neighborhood, is almost all white and enrolls only girls. Students from the suburban high school, which was located in an upper-middle- to lower-upper-class neighborhood, were almost all white and the school was coeducational. In the parochial high schools, only juniors were studied.

*Instruments.* The adolescents in our study were asked to complete the Offer Self-Image Questionnaire (OSIQ); the Delinquency Check List (DCL) (Short and Nye, 1957), a self-report inventory of the extent of delinquent behaviors in which the subject has engaged; a survey of mental health services that the subject has used; and open-ended questions regarding problems and felt need for mental health services not received. A face sheet requesting demographic data, including parents' marital status, was also included. Questionnaires were given anonymously, but the respondents could write their names, addresses, and telephone numbers in a space provided for that purpose if they were willing to participate in future research. About 60 percent of all students studied indicated their willingness to participate in future research.

*Data Analysis.* OSIQ data were scored with a standard score format so that eleven OSIQ scale scores describing functioning in a variety of areas were obtained for participants. These OSIQ scores were then used as a criterion of disturbance. A student who scored one standard deviation or more below the mean (a score of 35 or less in standard score terms) on three or more OSIQ scales was considered disturbed. The number of disturbed students who were "quiet" — that is, who had not received professional help more than once, who had not been stopped or apprehended by the police more than once, and who had never by self-report committed any serious, highly visible delinquent act — was identified. Of the quietly disturbed adolescents, 50 percent had never seen any mental health professional at all. Analyses were also performed to determine the mean OSIQ scale scores for all male and female students, for male and female disturbed students, and for male and female quietly disturbed students.

## Results

Results show that 18 percent of the male students in the Chicago suburb and 17 percent of the students in the all-boys Chicago parochial school met our criterion of disturbance. Among female students, 13 percent of those in the Chicago suburb and 32 percent of those in the all-girls Chicago parochial school met our criterion of disturbance. Of these students, 33 percent of the disturbed boys and 66 percent of the disturbed girls were quietly disturbed, in the sense that they had not been stopped or apprehended by the police more than once; they had never engaged in any highly visible, serious delinquent act; and they had not been seen by a mental health professional more than once.

OSIQ scale score means for boys and girls are shown in Table 1. Results are well within the range of the normal according to OSIQ norms. In no case was a scale score mean as much as five standard score points below the norming group mean. The largest difference between OSIQ norms and the scores of the groups that we tested occurred with respect to the Sexual Attitudes scale. On that scale, the all-male, all-black parochial school had a mean standard score of 58, indicating that their sexual attitudes were somewhat more "liberal" than those of the norming group.

OSIQ scale score means for disturbed and quietly disturbed students are shown in Tables 2 and 3. For purposes of contrast, the reader may wish to compare the scale scores of identified psychiatrically disturbed groups reported

### Table 1. Offer Self-Image Questionnaire (OSIQ) Scale Score Means for Students from Three Chicago Area Communities

| OSIQ Scale | | Chicago Suburb (N = 102) | Chicago Parochial High School (N = 59) | Chicago Suburb (N = 100) | Chicago Parochial High School (N = 74) |
|---|---|---|---|---|---|
| PS-1 | Impulse Control | 55 | 53 | 51 | 50 |
| PS-2 | Emotional Tone | 51 | 53 | 51 | 47 |
| PS-3 | Body and Self-image | 51 | 53 | 53 | 48 |
| SS-1 | Social Relationships | 52 | 55 | 53 | 52 |
| SS-2 | Morals | 56 | 48 | 53 | 51 |
| SS-3 | Vocational-Educational Goals | 53 | 54 | 56 | 51 |
| SxS | Sexual Attitudes | 50 | 58 | 51 | 46 |
| FS | Family Relationships | 53 | 50 | 52 | 47 |
| CS-1 | Mastery of the External World | 53 | 50 | 53 | 48 |
| CS-2 | Psychopathology | 53 | 53 | 54 | 46 |
| CS-3 | Superior Adjustment | 54 | 54 | 56 | 51 |

Note: PS = Psychological Self, SS = Social Self, SxS = Sexual Self, FS = Familial Self, CS = Coping Self

in Chapter Five. Due to the method of selecting the disturbed and the quietly disturbed students, it is not surprising that their OSIQ scale score means are notably lower than those of the norming groups of students. However the mean scale scores of the disturbed and the quietly disturbed students are more than just lower than those of the normals. They are also similar to the scores of psychiatrically disturbed adolescents. In addition, there are some notable differences in the OSIQ scale scores of disturbed and quietly disturbed youths.

### Table 2. Offer Self-Image Questionnaire (OSIQ) Scale Score Means for Disturbed and Quietly Disturbed Males

| OSIQ Scale | | Disturbed (N = 18) | Quietly Disturbed (N = 9) |
|---|---|---|---|
| PS-1 | Impulse Control | 32 | 49 |
| PS-2 | Emotional Tone | 36 | 33 |
| PS-3 | Body and Self-image | 35 | 30 |
| SS-1 | Social Relationships | 38 | 38 |
| SS-2 | Morals | 41 | 47 |
| SS-3 | Vocational-Educational Goals | 38 | 46 |
| SxS | Sexual Attitudes | 48 | 33 |
| FS | Family Relationships | 33 | 45 |
| CS-1 | Mastery of the External World | 36 | 32 |
| CS-2 | Psychopathology | 33 | 37 |
| CS-3 | Superior Adjustment | 35 | 46 |

Note: PS = Psychological Self, SS = Social Self, SxS = Sexual Self, FS = Familial Self, CS = Coping Self

### Table 3. Offer Self-Image Questionnaire (OSIQ) Scale Score Means for Disturbed and Quietly Disturbed Females

| OSIQ Scale | | Disturbed (N = 12) | Quietly Disturbed (N = 23) |
|---|---|---|---|
| PS-1 | Impulse Control | 32 | 37 |
| PS-2 | Emotional Tone | 24 | 33 |
| PS-3 | Body and Self-image | 26 | 36 |
| SS-1 | Social Relationships | 37 | 37 |
| SS-2 | Morals | 44 | 44 |
| SS-3 | Vocational-Educational Goals | 42 | 44 |
| SxS | Sexual Attitudes | 45 | 42 |
| FS | Family Relationships | 26 | 42 |
| CS-1 | Mastery of the External World | 29 | 32 |
| CS-2 | Psychopathology | 29 | 36 |
| CS-3 | Superior Adjustment | 35 | 40 |

*Note:* PS = Psychological Self, SS = Social Self, SxS = Sexual Self, FS = Familial Self, CS = Coping Self

These results indicate that quietly disturbed male adolescents reported better impulse control, better family relationships, and a higher sense of competency than did disturbed boys who acted out, who had received help, or both. The quietly disturbed adolescents also reported notably more conservative sexual attitudes than the disturbed adolescents did. With respect to emotional tone, body image, social relationships, and mastery of external problems, the quietly disturbed males reported self-image as low as or lower than that of the disturbed male adolescents.

Quietly disturbed girls reported better emotional tone and markedly better family relationships than the disturbed girls did. Although the scores were not quite significant, quietly disturbed adolescent girls also attested to better body images than the disturbed girls did. In no scale did the quietly disturbed females evidence poorer functioning than the disturbed females did. On the social self scales—Social Relationships, Morals, and Vocational and Educational Goals—and on the sexual self scale—Sexual Attitudes—the results were virtually identical for the two groups.

### Discussion

As already noted, our data are consistent with previous epidemiological studies: About 20 percent of the adolescents in our study were emotionally disturbed to some degree. It has not been known until now what percent of disturbed adolescents have manifested this disturbance either through antisocial behavior sufficient to warrant apprehension by the police or by manifesting symptomatology disturbing enough to warrant treatment by a mental health professional. The data gathered in our study suggest that 50 percent of disturbed youths have not received significant help or come to the attention of authorities. It is of interest that the youths in our samples who were identified as disturbed have OSIQ profiles resembling those of youths who have been hospitalized for psychiatric illness. This fact suggests that the youths identified as disturbed in our samples have serious psychiatric problems.

Currently, there are about nineteen million adolescents in American high schools. Taking 15 percent as a conservative figure, our results suggest that approximately three million youths are emotionally disturbed. Again using a conservative estimate, our results suggest that one third of that number — about one million adolescents — are "quietly disturbed," meaning that they manifest significantly poor self-esteem and yet they do not receive professional help, and they do not come to the attention of law enforcement personnel.

Many disturbed adolescents, our data suggest, do not come to the attention of professionals either because they are not sufficiently disturbing to others or because the nature of their pathology precludes their reaching out for help. The few longitudinal studies show that disturbed adolescents tend to become disturbed adults (Doane and others, 1981; Vaillant and McArthur, 1972). Early intervention might save these individuals from many years of needless suffering. It might also save these individuals from perpetuating family pathology that can lead them to act in a pathogenic way toward the children that they have. With respect to these individuals, the burden may be on the mental health community. To treat these youths, the direct encouragement provided by participation and outreach programs may be necessary.

## References

Albert, N., and Beck, A. T. "Incidence of Depression in Early Adolescence: A Preliminary Study." *Journal of Youth and Adolescence,* 1975, *4,* 301–307.

Bjornsson, S. "Epidemiological Investigation of Mental Disorders of Children in Reykjavik, Iceland." *Scandinavian Journal of Psychology,* 1974, *15,* 244–254.

Csikszentmihalyi, M., and Larson, R. *Being Adolescent.* New York: Basic Books, 1984.

Doane, J. A., West, K. L., Goldstein, M. J., Rodnick, E. H., and Jones, J. E. "Parental Communication Deviance and Affective Style." *Archives of General Psychiatry,* 1981, *38,* 679–685.

Graham, P., and Rutter, M. "Psychiatric Disorder in the Young Adolescent: A Follow-up Study." *Proceedings of the Royal Society of Medicine,* 1973, *66,* 58–61.

Gurin, G., Veroff, J., and Feld, S. C. *Americans View Their Mental Health.* New York: Basic Books, 1960.

Kandel, D. B., and Davies, M. "Epidemiology of Depressive Mood in Adolescents." *Archives of General Psychiatry,* 1982, *39,* 1205–1212.

Krupinski, J., Baikie, A. G., Stoller, A., Graves, J., O'Day, D. M., and Polke, P. "A Community Health Survey of Heyfield, Victoria." *Medical Journal of Australia,* 1967, *54,* 1204–1211.

Langner, T. S., Gersten, J. C., and Eisenberg, J. G. "Approaches to Measurement and Definition in Epidemiology of Behavior Disorders: Ethnic Background and Child Behavior." *International Journal of Health Services,* 1974, *4,* 483–501.

Leslie, S. A. "Psychiatric Disorder in the Young Adolescents of an Industrial Town." *British Journal of Psychiatry,* 1974, *125,* 113–124.

Locksley, A., and Douvan, E. "Problem Behavior in Adolescents." In E. Gombera and V. Frank (Eds.), *Gender and Disordered Behavior.* New York: Brunner/Mazel, 1979.

Offer, D., Ostrov, E., and Howard, K. I. *The Adolescent: A Psychological Self-Portrait.* New York: Basic Books, 1981.

Rosenberg, M. *Society and the Adolescent Self-Image.* Princeton, N.J.: Princeton University Press, 1965.

Rutter, M., Graham, P., Chadwick, O. F. D., and Yule, W. "Adolescent Turmoil: Fact or Fiction?" *Journal of Child Psychology and Psychiatry,* 1976, *17,* 35–56.

Schoenbach, V. J., Kaplan, B. H., Wagner, B. H., Grimson, R. C., and Edry, J. R. "Depressive Symptoms in Young Adolescents." *Society for Epidemiologic Research: Abstracts,* 1980, *112,* 440.

Short, J. F., Jr., and Nye, F. I. "Reported Behavior as a Criterion of Deviant Behavior." *Social Problems,* 1957, *5,* 207–213.

Vaillant, G. E., and McArthur, C. C. "Natural History of Male Psychological Health I: The Adult LIfe Cycle from Eighteen to Fifty." *Seminars in Psychiatry,* 1972, *4,* 4–16.

Veroff, J., Kulka, R. A., and Douvan, E. *Mental Health in America.* New York: Basic Books, 1981.

*Eric Ostrov is director of forensic psychology in the Department of Psychiatry at Michael Reese Hospital and Medical Center and research associate (assistant professor) in the Department of Psychiatry at the University of Chicago Pritzker School of Medicine.*

*Daniel Offer is chairman of the Department of Psychiatry at Michael Reese Hospital and Medical Center and professor of psychiatry at the University of Chicago Pritzker School of Medicine.*

*Shirley Hartlage is a doctoral student in the Department of Psychology at Northwestern University.*

*The adolescent experience is shaped in part by cultural changes and historical influences.*

# Historical Time and Social Change in Adolescent Experience

Andrew M. Boxer
Harold P. Gershenson
Daniel Offer

Are adolescents of the 1980s markedly different from adolescents of the 1960s or of other decades? Some social scientists have suggested that those born during the baby boom of 1946–1963 will have gone through pressures and strains, while the generations preceding have had a disproportionately easier life experience (Easterlin, 1980; Hauser, 1980). Others suggest that there has been a decrease in life satisfaction for the youth of 1976 as compared to those of 1957 (Veroff and others, 1981). Still other data suggest that adolescents' self-images have changed, when adolescents of the early 1960s are compared to adolescents of the late 1970s (Offer, Ostrov, and Howard, 1981). In a recent longitudinal study of adolescents and their parents (Boxer and others, 1984), the

Preparation of this chapter was facilitated by predoctoral fellowships awarded to Andrew M. Boxer and Harold P. Gershenson by the Clinical Research Training Program in Adolescence, which is jointly sponsored by the Department of Psychiatry, Michael Reese Hospital and Medical Center; the Committee on Human Development, University of Chicago; and the Adolescent Program of the Illinois State Psychiatric Institute under the National Institute of Mental Health Training Grant MH14669.

D. Offer, E. Ostrov, K. I. Howard (Eds.). *Patterns of Adolescent Self-Image.* New Directions for Mental Health Services, no. 22. San Francisco: Jossey-Bass, June 1984.

parents were asked to compare their own youth to that of their adolescent children. Their common sense logic and everyday experience would have us believe that things are both different and the same. Yet the passage of time and accompanying social changes provide an ever-changing context in which development takes place. If adolescents of different eras do not change, the events and preoccupations that may inform their experience are surely changing, as a catalogue of political events affecting youth illustrates (see Table 1).

In this chapter we will examine demographic changes among adolescents in the United States and investigate how these changes vary by sex and race. Given the various hypotheses about recent changes in the experience of youth, as well as such major events as the Vietnam War, it seems essential to define the parameters of youth groups with the widest possible lens and to build descriptive elaborations of them based on basic demographic indicators such as age, sex, and race. In addition, the social characteristics of adolescents define the reference groups with which adolescents identify, in whole or in part, and sensitize us to the range of diversity among adolescents in contemporary society. However, we shall first turn our attention to a brief review of some major historical changes which have been thought to characterize the experience of youth.

### Time, Age, and History Among Adolescents

Social scientists who study the life span have increasingly focused their attention on differentiating those behaviors that are age related (and in this sense developmental) and those that may result from the impact of sociohistorical and cultural events (Schaie, 1965; Schaie and Hertzog, 1982). True developmental changes are those that are universal and that occur across diverse cultures and historical periods. To separate age and period effects, elaborate designs are required that are often beyond the possibilities of most research budgets. However, most studies of adolescent development typically do not address the historical and ecological factors that give shape to the context within which development occurs (see Elder, 1980). One remarkable exception to this is the study of personality development conducted by Nesselroade and Baltes (1974). Their study examined 1,800 children born between 1954 and 1957. Respondents in this study were tested three times during a two-year period. Developmental changes in personality were found to be more influenced by historical effects than by ontogenetic, age-related changes. However, the authors did not elaborate the specific contextual or historical factors that led to the resulting changes in personalilty that they delineated. The implications of this study have been directed largely to issues of method, rather than to substantive issues of defining particular sociohistorical forces that have an influence on the life course of youth.

The concept of cohort is central to understanding how members of a generation respond to sociohistorical circumstances (Cain, 1964, 1967; Ryder, 1965; Riley, 1976). However, a major problem is definition of a cohort.

Table 1. Significant Socio-Political Events Influencing Youth: 1900–1980

| Temporal Period | Decisive Political Events | Youth Movements |
|---|---|---|
| 1900–1929 | Economic growth and cultural liberalism Industrialization: United States develops favorable balance of trade and becomes world industrial power World War I Isolationism Prohibition Women's suffrage "Roaring Twenties" | Youth cultural challenges Victorian social and sexual mores |
| 1930–1940 | Great Depression Poverty Election of F.D.R.: "New Deal" Government economic programs Growth of Nazism in Germany | Youth join antiwar movement Youth sign Oxford Pledge Campus strikes |
| 1941–1949 | World War II Truman administration Atomic bomb Returning GIs Global reconstruction; United Nations | Little youth movement activity |
| 1950–1959 | The Cold War; Eisenhower years Growth of military industrial complex Dulles foreign policy Recession McCarthyism 1954 Supreme Court desegregation decision House Un-American Activities Committee | The "silent generation" |
| 1960–1968 | Kennedy–Johnson years "New Frontier" Civil rights demonstrations Peace Corps and poverty programs Vietnam War escalates Assassinations of Kennedy brothers and Martin Luther King "Great Society" programs Ghetto riots and campus disruption | New Left New Right Civil rights and black power Protest demonstrations, strikes, violence |
| 1969–1976 | Nixon–Ford Years Emphasis on law and order Voting Rights Act Vietnam War ends Kissinger foreign policy Inflation, job squeeze Growth of multinational corporations Watergate OPEC and Middle East oil embargo | Women's rights Ecology movement Charismatic religious movements Quiet seventies |

## Table 1. Significant Socio-Political Events Influencing Youth 1900–1980
### (continued)

| Temporal Period | Decisive Political Events | Youth Movements |
|---|---|---|
| 1977–1980 | Carter years | "No Nuke" movement |
| | Conciliatory, practical, informal mood in White House | Gay liberation |
| | Emphasis on reorganization of government | |
| | National energy crisis | |
| | Inflation, job squeeze | |
| | Iranian hostage crisis | |
| | Camp David accords | |
| | Three Mile Island | |

*Source:* Adapted from Braungart (1980).

The determination of the parameters of a cohort and the particular socio-historical events that are significant to a generation are as yet little understood (Cain, 1967). Studies in which data are analyzed by cohorts often determine the groups included in a given cohort by somewhat arbitrary criteria. It is clear that lives occur in the context of those events that assume particular significance and meanings for individuals. But it has been difficult for investigators to include such events in systematic research, with the exception of the work of Elder (1980).

Elder (1974, 1980) examined the impact of the Great Depression on the lives of children whose families experienced a one third drop in income during that period. Elder has demonstrated in a compelling way that the Depression had a particular impact on the lives and personalities of adolescent boys and girls that was different than the impact on those who were small children. Tracing the effects of this historical experience on adolescents' lives, Elder (1980) found that the adult life course of those who were adolescents during the Depression is somewhat different than for those who had been small children during that time. Thus, understanding adolescents in their historical and social context provides a more informed understanding of the course of development both prospectively and retrospectively.

The division of the life cycle into particular stages or periods is a culturally based phenomenon and is strongly affected by cultural systems (Hagestad and Neugarten, in press; Levine, 1978). The cultural meanings that are ascribed to various phases of biological development appear to be largely hinged on socially shared age-based definitions (Hagestad and Neugarten, in press). These meanings structure individuals' behavior with regard to privileges, obligations, rights, and accompanying role expectations. Examining patterns of development within specific sociohistorical contexts has come to be termed the life-course approach (Clausen, 1972; Elder, 1975). In this sense, adolescence is regulated by sociocultural phenomena that help give shape to life experience and may alter particular patterns of development.

Often adolescence is considered an unalterable period of life that is etched in stone. Investigators who study particular phenomena, such as identity development, expect their findings to remain stable across time periods and ignore the cultural and historical context within which identity is developed. Definitions of adolescence are themselves undergoing change, and there is an increasing number of divisions into early, middle, and late adolescence (Hamburg, 1974; Kagan, 1971; Thornburg, 1983). The age grading that occurs in school, for example, has increased the use of chronological age as a demarcation of social status and thereby accentuates the distinctiveness of subgroups of adolescents. Adolescence is therefore directly linked to social structure and to systems of age stratification and age status (Cain, 1964; Foner and Kertzer, 1979; Neugarten and Moore, 1968; Neugarten and others, 1965).

Social commentators have argued that the period of the life cycle we call childhood is slowly being transformed (Postman, 1982; Sommerville, 1982; Winn, 1983). Parents are unable to protect children effectively from the harsh realities of everyday life, one of the arguments states. Children must then accede to the demands of the adult world by becoming precocious and they lose the innocence of their childhood. While such arguments have not been supported with systematic developmental data, the periods of adolescence and youth have recently been subject to more scientifically based examinations of how history and social change may have altered and reorganized these periods of life. Some, including social scientists and policy makers, have argued that the period of youth has been moved forward in the life cycle, is protracted, and at the same time promotes alienation from the adult world (Coleman and others, 1974).

Michael Katz (1975) studied data from a mid-nineteenth century Canadian city and found that in the transition to adulthood most young people passed through a semi-autonomous state, having entered some adult statuses but not having completed the entire set of transitions into adulthood. The length of this period of transition appeared to be responsive to local economic conditions, becoming less apparent during periods of economic scarcity. Kett's (1977) study of the history of adolescence in the nineteenth century indicates that the experience of youth, especially rural youth, was not brief but was consistently filled with adult-like responsibilities. Regulated patterns of transition were not in evidence. During this historical period, the life cycle of youth was unpredictable and not well-ordered. Thus, these authors argue that the period of youth was somewhat protracted historically and much less predictable than is found among youth of today.

The most compelling set of data that support this finding is found in the study by Modell and others (1976). Their aim was to test the commonly held assumption that it has become more difficult to grow up because the passage to adulthood has become less clearly charted. Protracted schooling, economic dependency on the family, and the complex nature of career decisions are often taken to suggest that the timing of the transition to adulthood has become more prolonged and the sequence of changes less clearly prescribed. In their study, these investigators drew on contemporary census data and data collected from an 1880 Philadelphia Federal Population Manuscript Schedule. The primary limitation of this data was that it was restricted to white populations only. One of the investigators' more remarkable findings was that while most people who eventually marry now do so by their late twenties, a substantial proportion of females and most of the males a century ago did not wed until their late twenties or early thirties. Growing up in contemporary America, it was concluded, has become less prolonged, and the sequence of transitions including departure from the family of origin, marriage, and establishment of an independent household has become more concentrated. Although proportions of persons experiencing the various statuses have remained roughly the same in both centuries, there were significant changes in the spread and timing of transitions. For example, the two nonfamilial transitions (school exit and work-force entry) started earlier in the nineteenth century and required less time to reach completion. By contrast, in 1970 the transition to adulthood was accomplished earlier and in fewer years. Individuals today may have to make a number of more complex career decisions sooner (Modell and others, 1976).

These studies taken together suggest that the life course was less prescribed and defined for those growing up in the nineteenth century. Today the life course is more prescribed and predictable; this has been called an "average expectable life cycle" (Neugarten, 1979). Young people today must negotiate a more complex set of decisions about the sequence of events in the transition to adulthood (Hogan, 1982; Modell and others, 1976). Such decision making may itself be a source of stress (Hogan, 1982; Pearlin, 1980). Modell and others (1976) contrast a young man or woman in Philadelphia in 1880—who would enter the work force and contribute to the income of his or her family of origin for approximately seven years—with the family economy of 1970, which is dependent only on husband and wife income. Many children do not typically contribute to their families of origin but spend their money on consumer goods or create savings for their own families (Modell and others, 1976; Oppenheimer, 1974, 1981).

There are many nonfamilial institutions that are part of the transition to adulthood (Demos, 1979; Skolnick, 1979), particularly those relevant to education and training. Nineteenth-century individuals, once they were able to live up to familial obligations, may have had greater latitude in life course planning. Growing up, it is argued (Modell and others, 1976), has become briefer and "more normful, bounded, and consequential and thereby more demanding on the individual participants" (p. 31).

While the constraints of age appear to be taking on less significance generally (Neugarten, 1979), it has been argued that the early part of adulthood is more clearly age-graded now than was the case in the nineteenth century (Hogan, 1982; Neugarten and Hagestad, 1976; Hagestad and Neugarten, in press). The system of age-graded expectations (Neugarten and others, 1965) by which individuals come to anticipate particular life events constrained by age has become more predictable for adolescents while during other phases of the life course such age-based expectations may decrease. Hogan (1982) found that adolescents normally prefer to traverse the life course in the order of school, work, and marriage. However, there are decreasing proportions who follow this order and a larger number of diverse sequencing patterns found among youth (Hogan, 1982). Abeles and others (1980) examined data from Project Talent and found through path analyses that there were a variety of life patterns with school, career, and family interwoven among late adolescents and young adults.

## Demographic Changes Among Adolescents

Before describing changes observed over recent decades for adolescent populations, it is notable that there have been many historical changes that dramatically affect family life for all members, including adolescents. Uhlenberg (1978) has delineated a number of these changes that occurred between 1850 and 1950. An important variable affecting the family environment is the size of the unit itself. Larger families of orientation for earlier cohorts suggests that there were not only more children, but greater changes within the family as individuals progressed through the course of life. The family has become a smaller unit with less disruption caused by the death of a parent (Uhlenberg, 1978). In addition, for adult females, the child-rearing span has become shorter and the probability of divorce has increased. While a larger proportion in more recent age groups has been divorced by old age, a lower percentage have been widowed and a lower percentage never marry. An increasing proportion of the population lives out the course of life in a family context, which may have particular psychological as well as social consequences for adolescents.

In examining specific demographic changes for adolescent age groups in the United States population, we illustrate the hypothesis that the social and psychological experiences of adolescents have continued to change over recent decades. Those children born in the first wave of the baby boom between 1946 and 1950 became teenagers in the early 1960s, and the social upheavals of that decade were part of the adolescent experience. Those born during the peak of the boom between 1955 and 1959 became the post-Watergate and post-Vietnam generation of youth. The current cohort of teenagers was born after the Kennedy assassination (1963), the Civil Rights Movement (circa 1960), and the "summers of love" in 1966 and 1967. This generation is coming into adulthood during a period of economic recession, reductions in federal support for social programs, and increased world tension. The changes in social and political worlds are reflected in social indicators that illustrate changing parameters for adolescents. School attendance, labor force participation, sexual behavior, and even causes of death have changed for adolescents within the past twenty-five years.

Age is not the only determinant of an adolescent's situation in the social system, however. Both sex and race are also related to access to a job or education and to the cause of death. Historical change often interacts with sex, race, or both. Therefore, the data are contrasted for males, females as well as minorities and whites.

Most of the data come from information collected periodically by the federal government. Because of changes in reporting methods over time and differences in definitions and methods of reporting by different federal agencies, data across sections are not always strictly comparable. Age breakdowns vary, and information on minorities sometimes refers to nonwhites and sometimes to blacks. The number of years included also varies. All data that are graphed begin when possible with 1960 and continue to the most recent year for which published data are available. This variation, however, does not limit the ability to discern historical change among cohorts of adolescents. Readers interested in comparisons with other age groups are referred to the original sources. Care must be taken when comparing figures, because limitation of size prevents them from being drawn to the same scale.

The dimensions of the adolescent population were sharply altered as the infants of the baby boom reached maturity throughout the 1960s and 1970s. As illustrated in Figure 1, the population of ten- to fourteen-year-olds rose from 16.9 million in the 1960s and peaked in 1971 when their numbers reached 21 million. The change in the 1960s among fifteen- to nineteen-year-olds was even sharper, since the 1960 and 1961 groups were still pre-baby boom adolescents. The subsequent cohorts mounted rapidly in size because of a snowball effect of ever increasing birth cohorts reaching older adolescence throughout the 1970s. The population of fifteen- to nineteen-year-olds peaked in 1979 at 21.4 million and began a sharp decline into the 1980s.

With the increase in cohort size, adolescents represented an increasing proportion of the population (Figure 2). Among ten- to fourteen-year-olds the proportion rose from 9.4 percent in 1960 to 10.2 percent in 1969. A decline during the 1970s in the proportion of younger adolescents to a low of 7.8 percent in 1982 reflects the rapid aging of the American population. This phenomenon created a shift in the mid 1970s from an adolescent population that consisted of predominantly younger adolescents to one that consisted of predominantly older adolescents. These became more visible as their proportion of the population increased from 7.4 percent in 1960 to 9.9 percent in 1977.

Since the vast majority of adolescents is white, changes among this group parallel those among the entire youth population. There was a decline, however, in the relative proportion of whites in the adolescent population from 87 percent in 1960 to 82 percent in 1982. The population of nonwhite adolescents shows an independent trend. The numbers of both younger and older nonwhite adolescents grew throughout the 1960s, but at a much slower rate than for white adolescents. However, the numbers of nonwhite adolescents remained relatively constant throughout the 1970s; the numbers of younger adolescents decreased, and that of older adolescents increased very slightly in the second half of the decade.

# Figure 1. Total Population (Millions) Adolescents 10-14, 15-19, by Race, 1960-1982

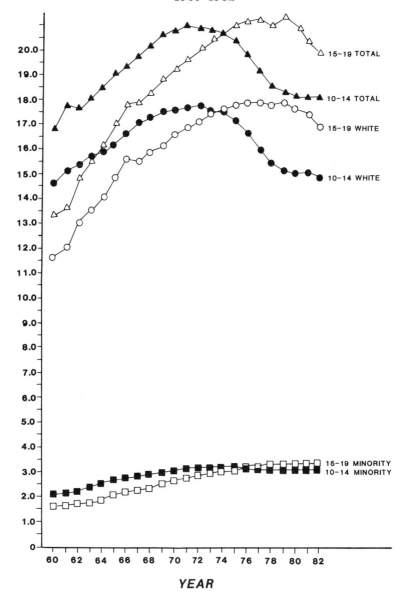

*Source:* U.S. Bureau of the Census, Current Population Reports, Series P-25, Nos. 929, 917, 614. U.S. Government Printing Office, Washington, D.C.

92

Figure 2. Percentage of Total Population, Adolescents Aged 10-14, 15-19
By Race, 1960-1982

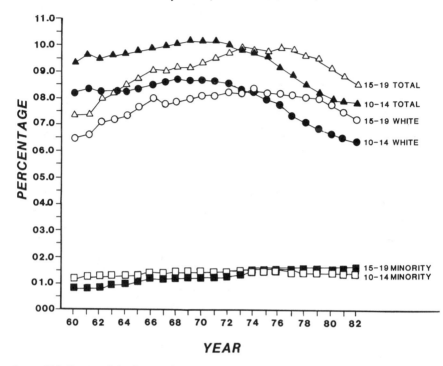

*Source:* U.S. Bureau of the Census, Current Population Reports, Series P-225, Nos. 929, 917, 614. U.S. Government Printing Office, Washington, D.C.

Sex differences are not illustrated because they are virtually nonexistent. In both decades, the white population has consistently been 49 percent female and 51 percent male for both younger and older adolescents. Among the nonwhite population, there have been equal numbers of males and females in both age groups.

Although it is easy to note the rapid increase in the adolescent population during the 1960s and to associate it with changes in adolescent culture and the rise of youth movements, examination of increasing racial differences belie any causal explanation between numbers in the population and cultural change. The civil rights movement, for instance, occurred during a period of only moderate increases in the minority adolescent population, and the movement declined as the population increased. The relationship of population size to cultural and social activity is perhaps better characterized as interactive. Increased numbers in any given age bracket provide a larger pool of potential participants in any ongoing cultural or political change. As they are drawn into the movement, their youth may alter its character.

## Summary and Discussion

As the country changes socially, politically, and economically, adolescents are faced with different conditions under which they will make the psychological and social transition from childhood to adulthood. While it is often debated whether adolescence is a construct of the twentieth century, it is frequently forgotten that the experience of adolescence today is in many ways markedly different from what it was five, ten, or twenty years ago. Adolescence is not simply a set of psychological transformations such as a growing sense of self or the acquisition of advanced cognitive skills. It is a set of transformations that are influenced by — and in turn influence — the world in which they take place.

Sociohistorical events do not affect all adolescents alike. As Elder demonstrated (1974), the impact of the Depression was dependent on the extent to which the adolescent's family suffered economic deprivation. Looking at recent cohorts of adolescents and distinguishing them by sex and race demonstrates the many ways this state of the life course has been experienced in recent years. Minority youth grew in numbers since 1960, but that growth has been insufficient to make a marked change in their proportion relative to the entire United States population.

These data demonstrate the range and diversity of adolescent social experience, and the accompanying historical changes that characterize it, and suggest numerous developmental patterns that may be found among various subgroups of youth. Rather dramatic changes over the last century have transformed the course of life and affected all members of society. Adolescence is generally a time when youth reorganize and conceptualize the future as well as the past (Boxer and others, 1984) as they move toward adult-like roles and responsibilities. As a result of shared social experience, individuals of particular ages at specific historical periods become members of a cohort or generation. They respond to the ecological milieu in ways uniquely determined by the interface of historical time, social structure, and life span (Elder, 1980). Examining the changing nature of adolescence in the life course sensitizes us to the experience of youth and adds to our understanding of the processes of growing up and growing old.

## References

Abeles, R. P., Steel, L., and Wise, L. "Patterns and Implications of Life Course Organization: Studies from Project Talent." In P. Baltes and O. G. Brim, Jr. (Eds.), *Life Span Development and Behavior.* Vol. 3, New York: Academic Press, 1980.

Boxer, A. M., Solomon, B. C., Offer, D., Petersen, A. C., and Halprin, F. "Parents' Perceptions of Young Adolescents." In R. Cohen, B. J. Cohler, and S. Weissman (Eds.), *Parenthood as an Adult Psychological Experience.* New York: Guilford Press, 1984.

Braungart, R. "Youth Movements." In J. Adelson (Ed.), *Handbook of Adolescent Psychology.* New York: Wiley, 1980.

Cain, L. "Life Course and Social Structure." In R. Faris (Ed.), *Handbook of Modern Sociology*. Chicago: Rand McNally, 1964.

Cain, L. "Age Status and Generational Phenomena: The New Old People in Contemporary America." *The Gerontologist*, 1967, *7*, 83–92.

Clausen, J. "The Life Course of Individuals." In M. Riley, M. Johnson, and A. Foner (Eds.), *Aging and Society*. Vol. 3. New York: Russell Sage Foundation, 1972.

Coleman, J. S., Bremner, R. H., Clark, B. R., Davis, J. B., Eichorn, D. H., Griliche, Z., Kett, J. F., Ryder, N. B., Doering, Z. B., and Mays, J. M. *Youth: Transition to Adulthood; Report of the Panel on Youth of the President's Science Advisory Committee*. Chicago: University of Chicago Press, 1974.

Demos, J. "Images of the American Family, Then and Now." In V. Tufte and B. Myerhoff (Eds.), *Changing Images of the Family*. New Haven, Conn.: Yale University Press, 1979.

Easterlin, R. A. *Birth and Fortune*. New York: Basic Books, 1980.

Elder, G. H., Jr. *Children of the Great Depression*. Chicago: University of Chicago Press, 1974.

Elder, G. H., Jr. "Age Differentiation and the Life Course." *Annual Review of Sociology*, 1975, *1*, 165–190.

Elder, G. H., Jr. "Adolescence in Historical Perspective." In J. Adelson (Ed.), *Handbook of Adolescent Psychology*. New York: Wiley, 1980.

Foner, A., and Kertzer, D. "Intrinsic and Extrinsic Sources of Change in Life Course Transitions." In M. Riley (Ed.), *Aging from Birth to Death: Interdisciplinary Perspectives*. Boulder, Colo.: Westview Press, 1979.

Hagestad, G. O., and Neugarten, B. L. "Age and the Life Course." In E. Shanas and R. Binstock (Eds.), *Handbook of Aging and the Social Sciences*. (2nd ed.) New York: Van Nostrand Reinhold, in press.

Hamburg, B. "Early Adolescence: A Specific and Stressful Stage of the Life Cycle." In G. Coehlo, D. A. Hamburg, and J. E. Adams (Eds.), *Coping and Adaptation*. New York: Basic Books, 1974.

Hauser, P. M. "Our Anguished Youth: Baby Boom Under Stress." In S. C. Feinstein, P. L. Giovacchini, J. G. Looney, A. Z. Schwartzberg, and A. D. Sorosky (Eds.), *Adolescent Psychiatry: Developmental and Clinical Studies*. Vol. 8. Chicago: University of Chicago Press, 1980.

Hogan, D. P. "Adolescent Expectations About the Sequencing of Early Life Transitions." Unpublished manuscript, 1982.

Kagan, J. "A Conception of Early Adolescence." *Daedalus*, 1971, *100*, 997–1012.

Katz, M. B. *The People of Hamilton, Canada West: Family and Class in a Mid-nineteenth Century City*. Cambridge, Mass.: Harvard University Press, 1975.

Kett, J. F. *Rites of Passage*. New York: Basic Books, 1977.

Levine, R. A. "Comparative Notes on the Life Course." In T. Hareven (Ed.), *Transitions: The Family and Life Course in Historical Perspective*. New York: Academic Press, 1978.

Modell, J., Furstenberg, F. F., Jr., and Hershberg, T. "Social Change and the Transition to Adulthood in Historical Perspective." *Journal of Family History*, 1976, *1*, 7–32.

Nesselroade, J. R., and Baltes, P. B. "Adolescent Personality Development and Historical Change: 1970–1972." *Monographs of the Society for Research in Child Development*, 1974, *39* (1), (entire issue).

Neugarten, B. L. "Time, Age, and the Life Cycle." *American Journal of Psychiatry*, 1979, *136*, 887–894.

Neugarten, B. L., and Hagestad, G. O. "Age and the Life Course." In R. H. Binstock and E. Shanas (Eds.), *Handbook of Aging and the Social Sciences*. New York: Van Nostrand and Reinhold, 1976.

Neugarten, B. L., and Moore, J. W. "The Changing Age-Status System." In B. L. Neugarten (Ed.), *Middle Age and Aging: A Reader in Social Psychology.* Chicago: University of Chicago Press, 1968.

Neugarten, B. L., Moore, J. W., and Lowe, J. C. "Age Norms, Age Constraints, and Adult Socialization." *American Journal of Sociology,* 1965, *90,* 710–717.

Offer, D., Ostrov, E., and Howard, K. I. *The Adolescent: A Psychological Self-Portrait.* New York: Basic Books, 1975.

Oppenheimer, V. K. "The Life Cycle Squeeze: The Interaction of Men's Occupational and Family Life Cycles." *Demography,* 1974, *11,* 227–245.

Oppenheimer, V. K. "The Changing Nature of Life Cycle Squeezes: Implications for the Socioeconomic Position of the Elderly." In R. W. Fogel, E. Hatfield, S. B. Kiesler, and E. Shanas (Eds.), *Aging: Stability and Change in the Family.* New York: Academic Press, 1981.

Pearlin, L. I. "Life Strains and Psychological Distress Among Adults." In N. J. Smelser and E. H. Erikson (Eds.), *Themes of Love and Work in Adulthood.* Cambridge, Mass.: Harvard University Press, 1980.

Petersen, A. C., and Boxer, A. "Adolescent Sexuality." In T. Coates, A. C. Petersen, and C. Perry (Eds.), *Promoting Adolescent Health: A Dialogue on Research and Practice.* New York: Academic Press, 1982.

Postman, N. *The Disappearance of Childhood.* New York: Delacorte Press, 1982.

Riley, M. "Age Strata in Social Systems." In R. Binstock and E. Shanas (Eds.), *Handbook of Aging and the Social Sciences.* New York: Van Nostrand Reinhold, 1976.

Ryder, N. "The Cohort as a Concept in the Study of Social Change." *American Sociological Review,* 1965, *30,* 843–861.

Schaie, K. W. "A General Model for the Study of Developmental Problems." *Psychological Bulletin,* 1965, *64,* 92–107.

Schaie, K. W., and Hertzog, C. "Longitudinal Methods." In B. B. Wolman (Ed.), *Handbook of Developmental Psychology.* Englewood Cliffs, N.J.: Prentice-Hall, 1982.

Skolnick, A. "Public Images and Private Realities: The American Family in Popular Culture and Social Science." In V. Tufte and B. Myerhoff (Eds.), *Changing Images of the Family.* New Haven, Conn.: Yale University Press, 1979.

Sommerville, J. *The Rise and Fall of Childhood.* Beverly Hills, Calif.: Sage, 1982.

Thornburg, H. D. "Is Early Adolescence Really a Stage of Development?" *Theory into Practice,* 1983, *2,* 79–84.

Uhlenberg, P. "Changing Configurations of the Life Course." In T. Hareven (Ed.), *Transitions: The Family and the Life Course in Historical Perspective.* New York: Academic Press, 1978.

Veroff, J., Douvan, E., and Kulka, R. A. *The Inner American: A Self-Portrait from 1957 to 1976.* New York: Basic Books, 1981.

Winn, M. *Children Without Childhood.* New York: Pantheon, 1983.

*Andrew M. Boxer is a doctoral candidate at the University of Chicago and a research affiliate in the Department of Psychiatry at Michael Reese Hospital and Medical Center.*

*Harold P. Gershenson is assistant director of the Ounce of Prevention Fund in Chicago.*

*Daniel Offer is chairman of the Department of Psychiatry at Michael Reese Hospital and Medical Center and professor of psychiatry at the University of Chicago Pritzker School of Medicine.*

*The findings presented in this volume have implications for mental health professionals, teachers, and parents.*

# Epilogue

*Daniel Offer*
*Eric Ostrov*
*Kenneth I. Howard*

Adolescents are often perceived as difficult to treat psychiatrically. In part, this has been due to our inadequate understanding of the adolescent experience. Such understanding depends on investigations of normal and disturbed youth as well as on comprehension of the historical and cultural contexts in which adolescents grow up. Such investigations need to include the adolescents' view of themselves in their milieu as well as their parents' perceptions of their sons and daughters.

Mental health professionals underestimate how positive the adjustment of most teenagers is. Mental health professionals also may not be knowledgeable about disturbed adolescents who do not seek help. These facts imply that we need to undertake more psychiatric-epidemiological research about disturbed adolescents who are not psychiatric patients. Such studies have just begun. We have called these adolescents *quietly disturbed,* because their disturbance is internal and because it does not affect their external world. Epidemiological studies should provide mental health professionals with guidance about what they can expect in the range of the normal and about the likely characteristics of youth who need psychiatric help but who are afraid or unable to reach out for it.

Mental health professionals have an important position in our culture.

D. Offer, E. Ostrov, K. I. Howard (Eds.). *Patterns of Adolescent Self-Image.* New Directions for Mental Health Services, no. 22. San Francisco: Jossey-Bass, June 1984.

Society often looks to them for expert advice about human feelings, behavior, and development. They are consulted not only for their expertise on psychopathology and psychotherapy but also for their knowledge of normal behavior and development. How close do the experts come in predicting what normal adolescents actually feel and think? We have found that mental health professionals are not very familiar with the extensive empirical literature on normal adolescent development (Offer, 1969; Masterson, 1967; Douvan and Adelson, 1966; Grinker and others, 1962; Werner and Smith, 1982; Brooks-Gunn and Petersen, 1983; Adelson, 1980; Offer and others, 1981), and they do not rely on it. This is unfortunate. It becomes particularly problematic when psychotherapists who have no clear notion of normality must help disturbed individuals to return to normal functioning (Offer and Sabshin, 1984). Our findings imply that courses on normal development are important for mental health professionals. It is also important for professionals to receive continuing education and to familiarize themselves with the current empirical literature; these measures could serve to balance their experience with the disturbed individuals who seek their help.

Parents and teachers also need to be educated. They should be aware that the vast majority of teenagers are well adjusted. They should also be aware of the special vulnerabilities of some adolescents, for example, some normal teenage girls. Becoming aware of adolescents' feelings and thoughts will help parents and teachers to become better able to relate to them. A good relationship depends on the ability of both participants to know and appreciate the other's uniqueness. Data show that, as the communication between parents and their adolescent children improves, the adolescents' self-image improves (Offer and others, 1982). Parents and teachers who are not aware of adolescents' feelings and who believe that problematic behavior is part of being a "typical" teenager may create two problems. First, they may not be able to have a close relationship with the child, because they feel no need to discuss specific issues with the child. Second and even more important, they may not be sensitive to the adolescent's need for professional help. Our findings indicate that, when an adult explains that the reason for a teenager's problematic behavior is that the adolescent is "just going through a stage," the teenager most probably needs professional help.

Examples of the kind of information that can be gleaned from research with adolescents abound in this volume. Chapter Two makes clear that, throughout the junior high school years, girls have poorer self-images than boys do, especially in the areas of emotional tone, body image, and coping. These results replicate those of Offer and others (1981), who showed that adolescent girls of high school age describe themselves as being sadder, lonelier, and more vulnerable than boys of the same age do. The girls also reported feeling worse about their bodies, and they had less faith in their own coping ability than the boys did.

These findings imply that many teenage girls need help with their body image and self-confidence. For adults who work with teenagers and for parents, a special sensitivity to the needs of teenage girls seems indicated. It may be helpful for girls who have difficulties in these areas to know that they are not the only ones who do. Becoming aware of the cultural and historical influences that shape these self-feelings and seeking ways to make changes when possible might also allow some of these girls to feel better about themselves.

Two chapters in this sourcebook present data showing that DSM-III diagnostic categories for adolescents can be supplemented by structured assessment of the adolescents' self-image. Necessarily, DSM-III focuses on specific sets of symptoms. However, adolescents who suffer from a particular psychiatric disease experience more than the symptoms of that disease. Having a psychiatric illness affects how adolescents think and feel about themselves in many areas. The same thing has been found to be true of adolescents who suffer from physical diseases (Offer and others, 1984).

The psychotherapist who treats disturbed adolescents confronts a series of obstacles. Parents may face similar obstacles in relating to their teenage sons and daughters. We have already discussed the problem of diagnosis — the problem of recognizing mental illness. In addition, since the psychotherapist or parent was an adolescent during a different sociohistorical period, the psychotherapist or parent had a very different adolescent experience and thus may have difficulty empathizing with the adolescent today. Such difficulty inhibits the formation of a close alliance and thus interferes with parenting or with providing psychotherapy. For many psychotherapists, relations with disturbed adolescents may be affected by the fact that they themselves were unhappy during their teenage years (Cremerius, 1983). Unfortunately, the therapist's memory of adolescence as an unhappy period may lend support to the therapist's tendency to view adolescence as a time of normative turmoil. To be effective, psychotherapists must not only have a realistic view of the normal adolescent experience, but they must also be able to understand how their patients experience themselves in the salient sectors of their lives. An understanding of the various aspects of adolescents' self-image is an essential component of such understanding, and it should facilitate a nurturing relationship between adults and adolescents.

## References

Adelson, J. (Ed.). *Handbook of Adolescent Psychology.* New York: Wiley-Interscience, 1980.
Brooks-Gunn, J., and Petersen, A. C. (Eds.). *Girls at Puberty.* New York: Plenum, 1983.
Cremerius, M. Personal communication, 1983.
Douvan, E., and Adelson, J. *The Adolescent Experience.* New York: Wiley, 1966.
Grinker, R. R., Sr., Grinker, R. R., Jr., and Timberlake, J. "A Study of 'Mentally Healthy' Young Males (Homoclites)." *Archives of General Psychiatry,* 1962, 6, 405.
Masterson, J. F., Jr. *The Psychiatric Dilemma of Adolescence.* Boston: Little, Brown, 1967.
Offer, D. *The Psychological World of the Teenager: A Study of Normal Adolescent Boys.* New York: Basic Books, 1969.

Offer, D., Ostrov, E., and Howard, K. I. *The Adolescent: A Psychological Self-Portrait.* New York: Basic Books, 1981.

Offer, D., Ostrov, E., and Howard, K. I. "Family Perceptions of Adolescent Self-Image." *Journal of Youth and Adolescence,* 1982, *11,* 281–290.

Offer, D., Ostrov, E., and Howard, K. I. "The Self-Image of a Group of Physically Ill Adolescents." In R. W. Blum (Ed.), *The Disabled and Chronically Ill Adolescent.* New York: Grune & Stratton, 1984.

Offer, D., and Sabshin, M. (Eds.) *Normality and the Life Cycle.* New York: Basic Books, 1984.

Werner, E. E., and Smith, R. S. *Vulnerable but Invincible: A Study of Resilient Children.* New York: McGraw-Hill, 1982.

*Daniel Offer is chairman of the Department of Psychiatry at Michael Reese Hospital and Medical Center and professor of psychiatry at the University of Chicago Pritzker School of Medicine.*

*Eric Ostrov is director of forensic psychology in the Department of Psychiatry at Michael Reese Hospital and Medical Center and research associate (assistant professor) in the Department of Psychiatry at the University of Chicago Pritzker School of Medicine.*

*Kenneth I. Howard is professor of psychology at Northwestern University; professor of psychology at Northwestern University Medical School; senior research consultant in the Department of Psychiatry at Michael Reese Hospital and Medical Center; and senior research consultant at the Institute for Juvenile Research.*

# Index

## A

Abeles, R. P., 89, 93
Abelson, R. P., 41, 42
Abramowitz, R. H., 19-28
Adelson, J., 19, 27, 98, 99
Adjective Check List, 30
Adolescent Research Rund, 1n, 29n, 57n
Adolescents: background on, 83-84; definitions of, 87; demographic changes among, 89-92; depression and conduct disorders among, 45-56; diagnostic work with, 13-14; early, changes in self-image among, 19-28; epilogue on, 97-100; focal theory on, 20, 22; historical time and social change among, 83-95; increased interest in, 1; normal, self-image of, 5-17; obstacles to treating, 99; parents and teachers of, 98; population of, 90-92; and psychopathology, 57-71; quietly disturbed, 73-81; socio-political influences on, 85-86; summary of changes among, 93; time, age, and history among, 84-89; and transition to adulthood, 87-89
Albert, N., 75, 80
American Society for Adolescent Psychiatry, 1
Asp, C. A., 20, 26
Australia: depression in, 45; Offer Self-Image Questionnaire in, 6; quietly disturbed adolescents in, 74

## B

Bachman, J. G., 21, 27
Baikie, A. G., 80
Baltes, P. B., 22, 26, 84, 94
Bangladesh, Offer Self-Image Questionnaire in, 6
Banks, J., 70
Battle, J., 59, 70
Beck, A. T., 46, 47, 55, 60, 70, 75, 80
Beck Depression Inventory, 47, 60, 75
Bell, L. G., 40, 41
Belleza, F. S., 40, 41
Benlifer, V. E., 31, 41, 42

Berndt, D. J., 45-46, 61n, 63n, 65n, 67n
Berndt, S. M., 47, 55
Birrell, P., 42
Bjornsson, S., 74, 80
Block, J., 58, 70
Blos, P., 1, 5, 16, 19, 26
Blyth, D. A., 21, 22, 25, 26, 28
Body and self-image: and early adolescents, 23, 24, 25, 26; and mental health professionals, 34; and normal adolescents, 6, 7, 10, 11, 12, 13, 14, 15; and psychopathology, 61, 63, 64, 65, 66, 67; and quietly disturbed adolescents, 78, 79
Bower, G. H., 40, 41
Boxer, A. M., 28, 83-95
Boys: changes in self-image among, 23, 24; depression among, 62-63; normal, 9, 10, 11-15; quietly disturbed, 75, 77, 78, 79
Braungart, R., 86n, 93
Bremner, R. H., 94
Brennan, T. G., 14n, 59, 70
Briscoe, B., 1n
Bronson, G., 58, 70
Brooks-Gunn, J., 98, 99
Bunney, W. E., 55
Bush, R. M., 28
Byars, W. D., 47, 55

## C

Cain, L., 84, 86, 87, 94
Canada, transition to adulthood in, 87
Cantwell, D., 46, 54, 55
Carlson, G., 46, 54, 55
Carlton-Ford, S., 26
Carroll, J. S., 40, 42
Casper, R., 64, 66, 67, 70
Chadwick, O. F. D., 28, 81
Chambers, W., 46, 55
Chicago, University of, Committee on Human Development at, 83n
Chigier's data, 12
Chow, M., 1n
Clark, B. R., 94
Clausen, J., 86, 94
Cline, V. B., 31, 42